MW00769025

HAVE YOU EVER SPELLED DOG BACKWARDS?

The Result of a Journey Walking With Dogs

Written with the help of dogs
By
Steve Fentress
'A Companion'

Aventine Press

Cover Art by
Center Line Digital Printing, Elizabeth City N.C.

Published by Aventine Press
1023 4th Ave #204
San Diego CA, 92101
www.aventinepress.com

ISBN: 1-59330-522-2

Printed in the United States of America

DEDICATION
To
My Truest Companions

One of the reasons I wrote this book was to repay a debt, but I postponed writing this dedication until it was finished. I know that's like putting the 'sled before the dog', but I wasn't sure that my effort here would prove commensurate with the merit and nature of the dogs to whom this book is dedicated. And with the completion of this book, I realize the past and present members of this elite group remain short-changed. Even with this dedication, the scales remain unbalanced; for the proffer of this book is but a meager pittance, doing little to accomplish equilibrium. Therefore, a great debt remains unpaid to the companions who have lighted my way in this life. But ever true to their saintly character, graciously they will accept a simple gesture of *'thank you'* - and a belly rub - and mark the obligation satisfied. Such is the nature of dogs. Their names, unlike the few humans mentioned in this book, remain unchanged and are contained within its pages. Listing them here is unnecessary. But even as the print on theses pages fades away with time, their names will forever remain imprinted on my heart.

The Result of a Journey Walking With Dogs

"We need another and wiser and perhaps more mystical concept of animals. We patronize them for their incompleteness, for their tragic fate of having taken form so far below ourselves. And therein we err, and greatly err. For the animal shall not be measured by man. In a world older and more complete than ours they move more finished and complete, gifted with extensions of the senses we have lost or never attained, living by voices we shall never hear…" *

....unless we abandon our haughty prejudice and learn to communicate with their soul and submit to their guidance, following them as we travel together on our journey.

* Henry Beston

TABLE OF CONTENTS

PROLOGUE

"The completion of a journey of a thousand miles begins with the first step."   Old Chinese Proverb

'If you're reading this book it means you probably paid for it, which means it was published. And with its publication, I hope it reaches the hearts of a multitude of people, generating tremendous profits to be donated to the benefit of the book's protagonist: dogs. That's right, the proceeds, every bit, belong to homeless shelters to subsidize the expense of maintenance, spays and neuters, with the hope that the necessity of such places will cease to exist.'

When I started this book over two years ago, realizing the uncertainty of its publication, I began the first line with the tentative word – *If*. When publication became a reality, I thought about changing the opening line, but decided to leave it intact. But I am still not convinced of the book's worth or its reach. Only time and reader response will establish both. However, one thing is certain: as long as this book is in print, the proceeds from its sale will *'go to the dogs'*. Although many words and phrases in this book have been in a constant state of revision, the intent stated in the original and unrevised italicized words of the first paragraph remains unchanged, and forever shall be so.

You may have found this book in the spiritual/self-improvement department or on the companion-animal shelf. I figure it can be placed in one or the other, but I would rather see it in both, for it is about both. It concerns dogs, their noble traits, and their wonderful contribution to our humanity and their role as our guide on a journey. It is also about our path of spiritual development. It is about how we can improve our lives and the lives of those we touch, including the dog, if we recognize and emulate the true goodness and the amazing grace these admirable creatures demonstrate. I hope the following pages will open your eyes and hearts nudging you to accept the magnificent gifts dogs offer, helping you to recognize them as the blessing they truly are.

I hope that you'll receive this book in the true spirit it was written. It offers no scientific studies, no medical advice, no psychological examinations, and no exercises to train your dog to behave a certain way - or to adopt certain traits. It is about his innate, gracious character from which he never strays. And if you open your heart and mind as you read, I am sure you will come away with a deeper appreciation for his natural virtues and, perhaps, a better understanding of your own.

Chapter 1
PROTAGONIST AND PURPOSE

"The dog has the soul of a philosopher."   Plato

The virtuous, honorable character inborn in the dog represents the essence of moral fiber continually discussed and sought after by ancient and modern philosophers, theologians, and 'masters'. However most, if not all, conspicuously exclude any mention of the dog as the model for mankind's aspiration toward godliness. The dog personifies the qualities that self-help books urge us to seek out and emulate. Yet, the authors fail to credit canines as the linch-pin of the tenets their books discuss. The dog's fundamental nature demonstrates and underpins the premise of every altruistic sermon moralized by humans genuinely pronouncing truth and love, but seldom do they acknowledge the dog's attributes as the basis for their homily.

Notwithstanding the lack of distinction afforded the dog in these matters by the pundits, he remains the true incarnation and personification of love, truth, and joy, and a constant teacher of humility, forgiveness, tolerance, and loyalty. By 'divine design' the dog is destined to appear before us as a precious gift, one who patiently waits for our appreciation and our acceptance of the lessons he reveals. And this is what this book will explore and explain.

This book has two purposes, each equally important. First, to find and recognize God by revealing tangible evidence of His existence, introducing touchable, incontrovertible proof of God's presence in our everyday world, despite mankind's attempts to isolate and obfuscate Him. With the dog's help, we will find proof that God walks among us, rather than One who remotely presides over our lives promulgating edicts and laws down from a throne situated in an ethereal realm; and, from there, *only* communicating to a few *'chosen men'*. Second, I hope to convince as many people as possible that the dog, our nexus to God, walks among us as an indispensable guide who leads us to connect with the spirit of our soul. A creature worthy of esteem, not as a possession, but as an equal. A partner deserving our love and respect, and an exceptional treasure to be cherished and held dear. Hopefully, with a newfound appreciation, the dog will ascend in the hierarchy of your mind, compelling the symbiotic and simultaneous enhancement of *his* station and *your* spirituality.

I'm not a dog doctor, a dog psychiatrist, a dog nutritionist, or a dog trainer. I am a dog companion and I walk with dogs, traveling on a journey with them as my guide. And since the beginning of our walk and all along the way, they reveal themselves as the salient endowment from nature and the supreme gift from God. There may be other animals in the natural world that may possess the noble characteristics of our dogs, but we haven't domesticated them, or more precisely, they haven't bonded to us to the same degree.

The *dog's* leap from the wilderness of *wolf* ancestry to the domestic bond with humans is verified by empirical standards of the science of genetics and archeology. Each discipline documents the leap, labeling it an evolutionary aberration: one that flies in the face of Darwinist principals. Scientific evidence verifies that the dog completed the mysterious leap within the incredibly short time of about two hundred years, a span much too rapid for explanation by evolution, and much too swift for the science of genetics to comprehend. Nowhere in history has this unique, ongoing bond between two species been replicated and no union benefits man as extensively. Although much time has been devoted to study and many words written about this bond, the most important benefit of it remains ignored by many dog aficionados and anti-anthropomorphic scientists alike; and this often-neglected benefit is the foundation of this book.

The purpose of our individual journey through life from the time we are born is to grow, learn, and evolve. And collectively, history of our evolution traces our emergence from the cave to the trappings of our existence in the 21st-century. There exists a pervading impulse that steers society and the individual to aspire to climb out of the marshes of ignorance and evolve. Something is and has been afoot that compels our individual and collective growth: a mysterious force aside from man's pretentious religions and destructive ego. And part of our evolution as a species is to explore and explain this enigmatic force. It is requisite and, I think, part of God's plan that we do. The journey of evolution and spiritual growth must include a path to knowledge. Questions must be asked so answers may be found, and lines of communication must be opened even when the entity holding the answers is not speaking in terms of human language. Yes, there is a mystique about the bond between dogs and humans. The humble dog bonds to us, in purpose and function, as a noble teacher with lessons necessary for evolution and enlightenment. The source and cause of this mysterious bond, unexplained by human science or rationale, is what this book brings to light.

I believe this book represents a unique presentation of the character and purpose of dogs who walk among us as teachers and messengers. Contained in the following pages of this book some of you are likely to find concepts about dogs you may consider uncustomary. Concepts that to some readers might seem, if not far-fetched, at least somewhat unusual. To some readers the concepts and observations may seem completely logical and evident, and yet some may dismiss the premise of this book altogether proclaiming its contents radically dubious and anthropomorphic. But I believe it presents a truthful insight into the essence of our dogs without romanticizing or idealizing it. And I have tried to refrain from offering hypothesis and conjecture about the psychological workings of the dog's mind, while presenting outward, explicit, and clearly demonstrative traits of man's truest companion.

What you will not find on these pages is any reference to a dog as a possession. For no human owns these creatures. It has become common practice for humans to transfer a perceived commodity of value (money) to acquire ownership of another commodity of perceived equal value.

But this process or transaction of ownership only works involving vehicles, houses, and other inanimate things. And just as a man cannot claim ownership of another of his kind, nor can ownership be claimed over a dog. Neither will you find the word master as some humans like to proclaim themselves when they refer to their dog. The use and practice of that word, rightfully abolished in 1863, and the connotation of dominion and subservience it imposes, has the same haughty and demonic connotation when used to claim dominion over a dog. We are not their owners, and we are not their masters, even in the benign sense of the word meaning 'teacher'; and we lack the capacity or the competence to be either. We are their companions. And they love us. They love us more than we love each other, and more than most of us love ourselves. And unfortunately, the fact is they love us more than we love them. As you finish this book, I hope you'll find reason within to challenge and change that statement of fact.

In the vein of insignificance on the other hand, the masculine gender of pronouns is used exclusively in this book. Primarily, because of my laziness and typographical shortcomings, I just didn't want to take the time or the effort to type a 'her' after every time I typed a 'his', or to be more politically correct, to type a 'his' after a 'her'. So you won't find equal-time expressed by using *his/hers* or *mankind/womankind* and other such overused, worn-out, politically correct phrases. Dogs don't bother with the trumped-up niceties of such antics and, frankly, neither should we.

On behalf of all dogs, especially the many suffering in ill-fated situations, I thank you for buying this book and helping the needs of man's truest and most devoted companion. Also, I sincerely hope this book, like the dog, helps light the path on your spiritual journey.

Chapter 2

WALKING WITH DOGS

"Every boy should have two things: a dog, and a mother willing to let him have one." Robert Benchley

The first thing I want to share with you as I write this portion of the book is that I have no earthly idea how to write a book at all. The majority of what follows on these pages either exists on haphazardly scattered pages and random notes, or survives in the file cabinet of my mind. After drudgingly committing words to paper in the form of a rudimentary manuscript, I let a chosen few individuals, who I knew would not be too critical, read parts while the book was in its infancy. I did so hoping that they would like what I had written so far and encourage me to continue. All were encouraging; but, knowing of my deep personal relationship with dogs, suggested that I relate stories of my personal experiences. I took their comments to heart, but this book will not contain anecdotal personal interactions with my dogs and many subsequent epiphanies that occurred. Had I done so, with so many stories to relate, this book would swell to the length of *"War And Peace"*, would be tedious to write and more tedious to read. It is my fervent hope that this book will urge you (nudge you) to embark on an individual journey that will ultimately lead you to personal growth and, most importantly, a profound spiritual admiration for dogs. My interactions with and love for my dogs are only important because these are things that caused me to write this book in the first place. But the comments so graciously given by my early readers do have merit. For you the reader to be comfortable with me the writer, you have to consider me a credible source, a source with a background with dogs.

It was early October 1959 when I picked out my first puppy from the litter of six pups residing in the house two doors down. I was eight years old when I carried the wriggling, black bundle of fur across my backyard to my house. What began as a parental effort to teach a youngster responsibility became an everlasting union between two friends (Smokey and me) who really needed and loved each other. I grew from a typical, somewhat selfish child, to a more self-absorbed teenager, and then to a young adult who 'knew it all'. Smokey, on the other hand, in a short time grew to a beautiful, longhaired, silky-coated, thirty-five-pound, black dog of mixed ancestry. Contained in his shell was the epitome of courage, selflessness, nobility, and undying love; all the things deep down I knew I wasn't. And deep down in my soul, I deeply respected and loved him knowing that he inherently possessed all the attributes I only pretended to have.

He was my constant companion. Everyday he walked with me to my elementary school, watched me enter, and satisfied with my safety, left for home only to return at the exact time school let out and walk me home. In later years when getting to school required bus trips, he saw me off and patiently waited for my return so we could take our daily journey through the forty acres near our house.

He flushing out and chasing rabbits and squirrels, and I attempting to figure out who I was and what dreams might come true. Fleetingly (being too naive and too egocentric to fully understand) I would marvel at his simplistic goodness, nobility, and love so unselfishly offered. Because of my pretentious, self-absorbed, false reality of life, I paid little attention to the 'snapshot' of his soul and character. Neither did I recognize the extent his comparatively short life would contribute, like all the dogs who followed, to the ultimate, total picture of my life and understanding; and, the reason for this book. My beloved Smokey died of old age in the summer of 1977, one month short of his eighteenth birthday.

July 10, 1981 - my oldest son's eleventh birthday. I decided it was time he and his eight-year-old brother should have an opportunity to try their hand at animal husbandry, with all its attendant responsibilities. Little did I know this day would set the stage for all my future dog dramas. We headed to a mall that I vaguely remembered contained a pet store. I use the term vaguely since I only stole furtive glances at the place while I quickly walked past, never daring to enter. I knew that my heart would be snared with only one glance at the adorable inhabitants, their tails joyously wagging while standing on their back legs, front paws frantically pawing the Plexiglas that cruelly separated us. I was keenly aware that had I ever walked into this place I would have walked out with a loving bundle of fur gratefully licking my face, thanking me for removing him from his confining world of plastic and cold steel. A place artificially lit by day with ice-bright fluorescent lights, and a place where the nighttime held only two things: darkness and loneliness. No, I never dared to walk into such a place. At this time, long workdays meant pandering myself to the corporate world, and nights were devoted to all the willing women I could find. Such behavior did not allow for, nor did it deserve, the companionship and love of a dog. But I would like to digress for just a few seconds.

I should note that at this time in my life I naïvely supposed that a pet store was the best place to go if you were looking for a dog. A dog born to parents lovingly cared for by humans who allowed the litter to be born mainly to satisfy all the adoring humans who would eventually be standing on the opposite side of the Plexiglas. It was five years later when I first learned of the term 'puppy mill'. Those two words in the form of a noun is a horrible place, and in verb form is a hideous practice, representing the epitome of man's greed made even more contemptible and damnable by his cruelty. The noble and loving dogs are nothing but expendable commodities whose only purpose is to breed. When they are sick with congenital diseases or from the horrible living conditions, and no longer able to fulfill the quota of pups every six months, they are killed and disposed of like trash. A despicable and unfair life for a creature far more noble than the human profiteers who call themselves 'breeders'. Many pet stores are the profit centers and the clearinghouses for the results of the puppy mills. Hopefully, one day neither the mills, nor the stores which sell their puppies, will exist.

But here we were: Two kids and one adult. The two excited kids exuberantly behaving like kids, and I embarrassingly behaving as if I were the youngest of the three. After meeting with several of the inhabitants of the cages, and dickering over the price of the one chosen, we left with a three-month-old Bichon Frise. An unfamiliar breed to me, but a breed I would come to know and dearly love.

The puppy who became known as Jock was loaded along with my boy's baggage and left with them on the trip back to Roanoke, Virginia, where the dog and my boys would live with their mother and stepfather for nine months until next summer's vacation. A year and a half passed until Christmas of 1982 rolled around necessitating a trip to Roanoke to deliver holiday presents and spend time with my boys. After watching my two children tear into the Christmas gifts, my ex-wife presented *me* with a present - Jock. "The boys don't pay any attention to him any more and he has to stay in the basement most of the time because he is loaded with fleas", she said. "We just don't think he's happy living here; so take him home with you." Looking around the living room I observed two cats, '*five star*' hotels for fleas, calmly lounging around on the furniture. Weakly, I said 'OK,' while wondering how in hell I was going to care for a dog. My business was six months old and I was struggling just to take care of me. Jock and I got into the car and began a journey: a journey not only back to Virginia Beach, but ironically, to where I now sit writing this, twenty-five years later.

In 1984, I found myself back in a pet store. This time I was looking for an anniversary present for my wife. Putting up with me through three years of dating and one year of marriage deserved either diamonds or gold, but I was in a pet store looking at a nice fish swimming in a gallon bowl. Needless to say, she was not overly enthused with her anniversary present. Two days later the fish died, so off we went to the mall so she could pick out a more suitable gift, one more commensurate with the time spent indulging my singularly egotistical behavior. We headed to the mall - she heading for the jewelry store and I back to the pet store. Over an hour later she found me in a cubicle with a three-month-old female Bichon Frise. Her voice raced as she feverishly started to describe the diamond necklace she had found. But as she looked into the face of the puppy I was holding, her description of the trinket seemed to go in slow motion. And then her voice, losing all of the excitement, slowed to a point that she never finished her sentence, realizing that a diamond necklace, sparkling and radiant as it may have been, paled in comparison to the big, brown eyes of the pure white puppy I had already named Mercedes. I didn't say a word and neither did she. We just walked out of the mall with a wonderful addition to our home and a playmate for Jock.

The words 'Until death do us part' did not become reality for me. As future years would teach me, that phrase would only apply in a dog's world. As my wife and I divorced, she wanted nothing that reminded her of me. So the three of us: Jock, Mercedes, and I left and set up house.

Mercedes developed into a shining example of the breed standard for the Bichon; quite an aberration of genetics for a dog produced by puppy mills. As I later found out by researching the breed, her coat, color, and size were perfect. Her large, deep dark brown eyes were expressive beyond description, and the dark black rim around the perimeter of her eyes gave the appearance of meticulously applied eyeliner. Women would kill for such eyes. All the right places were white and curly, and all the other places were dark and expressive. Jock had a looser, finer coat, but his eyes were just as expressive and dark. Both were fine dogs with endearingly sweet and loving dispositions.

It was 1986, the twenty-fifth of May, when a very apprehensive human witnessed Mercedes deliver five miracles of life. Two males were firstborn, followed by three females. The five arrivals came off without a hitch, except for the first female who decided to appear feet first, necessitating intervention by a nervous and inept midwife: me. By mid-afternoon all was quiet and serene. Pups found the comfort of nourishing milk. Jock, the sire, observed the scene from a distance, while Mom relaxed in her box. And a relieved human marveled at the sheer beauty and innocence of the miracle of newborn life and the immeasurable mystery of the event. A momentous event illustrating the continuity of life confirmed by the insignificant birth of five insignificant pups perpetuated by an insignificant mom and dad, and witnessed by an insignificant human. Outside the den where all this occurred, the world continued business as usual without even a thought concerning the miracle that happened on that insignificant day in May of 1986. For such miracles are ubiquitous throughout the world of nature and such things go unnoticed by all except the perpetrators who seemed unaffected by the miracle, and a human who will forever be moved by the simple, yet miraculous, event.

Several family trips were taken to the Vet during the next two months to monitor the progress of both mother and pups. All seemed to be in good health, except for the firstborn female who had developed a constant 'snotty' nose. Medication was administered and aside from this condition, which the Vet assured would clear, the family of seven dogs and one adult were enjoying the joyful experience of discovering the aftermath of the miracle and exploring the world of puppydom. After about two months amidst the happiness and playful antics, Mercedes started to tire of the constant trips to her box to comply with the growing intrusions of the insatiably hungry, rambunctious pups. The day of weaning was at hand much to the dismay and disillusionment of the pups. But Mercedes knew time had come to break the bonds of dependency. Little did she know that while the bond of dependency would be broken, her pups would remain and she would always be Mom.

During this time, Jock began to bump into things he should have easily avoided – like a closed door. A trip to the Vet brought the diagnosis of cataracts and glaucoma, a condition that manifested itself rapidly since his last exam six months prior. This condition necessitated a trip to N.C. State Veterinary Teaching Hospital in Raleigh, where subsequent surgery relieved the painful pressure on the eyes and restored limited vision to an almost totally blind dog. The operation was a success but I learned the gene, perpetuated by the unnatural and indiscriminate breeding practices at the puppy mills, had likely been passed on to the pups, and I had unknowingly allowed this terrible gene to survive. This carelessness, along with the hideous living conditions, is the true evilness of puppy mills. Reckless abandonment of integrity driven by greed, knowingly and indiscriminately, allows pernicious genes producing hip dysplasia, congenital heart disease, cataracts, and many others to exist in perpetuity. Even though I knew from the beginning that Mercedes, for the sake of her health, would produce only a single litter, both she and Jock were neutered to insure against the possibility of an accident and the further perpetuation of a cruel, abhorrent gene.

It had been four months since the birth. Jock was recovering from his surgery; and it was time to allow three of the pups to go on to their future homes. My father would eventually take two: the second born male, known as Pug so named for his short nose, and the firstborn female, Little Girl, the runt of the litter and the one with the snotty nose. Another female known as Bridget, the fourth born, was promised to a longtime friend and his daughter, my godchild. The three pups carried two stipulations: they must be spayed or neutered at the first safe opportunity, and if they developed cataracts, they must be allowed to have the operation to correct their vision. Two days before their departure, the whole family traveled to a photography studio for family portraits. Only one studio in town agreed to the photo session. The owner admitted that he had never photographed a family of dogs consisting of two nervous, uncooperative adults and five rambunctious, mischievous pups. After two hours of utter mayhem, he vowed never to do it again.

Little Girl and Pug proved to be the two best gifts ever received by my father. I watched as these two dogs conquered the timeworn heart of this sixty-eight-year-old man: a product of the Great Depression, a Pacific veteran of World War II, and a widower. The two pups found an avenue to this man's heart through love and tenderness. They adored him and he repaid their adoration with love, pure devotion, and concern for their well-being and safety. He gladly endured many trips to N.C. State Veterinary Teaching Hospital and the expense of treating Little Girl, whose perennial snotty nose indicated a serious and extremely rare congenital disease that attacked her lungs and immune system.

Within a couple of years, another Bichon entered my life. Phoebe was a three-month old companion of a human whose love for dogs was much more developed than my own at that time. Norma Jean and I began a lasting friendship made constant by a common denominator: dogs. Phoebe was a feisty, small Bichon who warmed only to a select few and I was one of the few. Full-time family now numbered four, and on a part-time basis, increased to five. In 1993 that changed. Norma Jean arrived unannounced at my house with two yapping, light-tan, four-legged things that remotely resembled dogs. They were apricot Toy Poodles in hideous condition, malnourished and obviously weak except for the outbreak of yapping and barking as they weakly climbed the steps to my house. Their coat, or rather what resembled it, was long and terribly matted. Their half-shut eyes were encrusted with dirt and mucus obviously obscuring their vision, but their vocal cords worked very well. She had been to the county pound and rescued these two ill-fated creatures who barely escaped euthanasia by the then common practice in this county of placing the poor creatures in a box and hooking a hose to the exhaust of a county vehicle. They had been stowaways on a tractor-trailer from Massachusetts whose driver, stopping at his appointed destination, discovered the two little Poodles hiding among his cargo. With loving care and several trips to the Vet, they cleaned up nicely. After two weeks, they finally stopped hunting and eating crickets, obviously their only source of nutrition for the first year or so of their malnourished life, and began concentrating on a more traditional dog menu. She kept the larger of the two, who became known as 'Biggit', and I kept 'Little It'. That made five for me and two for her. A total of seven when the two families were together, which was often since Norma Jean lived just down the street.

In 1994, October 7, my father suffered a fatal heart attack somewhere between the morning hours of eight and nine. There was no doubt as to the disposition of Little Girl and Pug. With their arrival that made seven. Now Mercedes had all but one of her pups again. But she took this in stride and so did the other four. One big happy family, until one morning when Pug, who had been playing in the yard with the others, ran past me through the kitchen into my bedroom and scooted under the bed. After several minutes, I went to check on this unusual behavior. From under the bed, I pulled out a dog, who, for no apparent health reasons, was dead. An exam by the Vet could not explain the death. X-rays showed no objects found ingested, no external or internal bleeding was evident. Nothing. That was on January 7, 1995, in the morning hour of 8:30, three months to the day after my father's death.

Several years passed before such devastation would visit our family again. On Good Friday, 1998, Mercedes, the love of my life, 'Sweet Mom' as she became known for tolerance and affection for her pups, left my pillow where she always slept, jumped from the bed and crawled under it letting out a whimpering yelp. From under the bed I retrieved a dog dying from a blood clot later determined to be caused by an operation on her throat two days prior. I later discovered the operation was a complicated, non-vital one that should have been performed, *if at all*, at a place better equipped to handle such a procedure, and completed by a surgeon more experienced with the intricacy of the operation, unnecessary as it was. She just turned fourteen and, except for a somewhat chronic cough caused by an age-induced, partial tracheal collapse, was a healthy dog. Six weeks later Little Girl, long suffering from the congenital disease attacking her lungs, her immune system damaged over the years, developed nasal cancer and left me three days after her twelfth birthday. That left four: Brutus, Portia, Little It, and Jock - who was now seventeen and completely blind from the cataracts surgery of years ago. His gait was slow, but his spirit indomitable.

Soon after Mercedes' premature death, Norma Jean arrived at my house with a plan she had concocted. She found a breeder in Long Island, New York who had four pups with champion lines - an inconsequential fact as far as I was concerned. She showed me a picture of the three-day old pups she had received: two males, two females. After much discussion in which she made her case for the necessity for me to have one of these pups, I adamantly refused to consider the proposition. Mercedes' death, for which I felt responsible, had devastated me. It was so unexpected and so untimely. The bond formed years ago at the birthing box would not soon, if ever, be replicated. Nor did I consider it possible at this time to bring a puppy into my life. As part of her argument as she was leaving, Norma Jean, dramatic to the end, walking out the door turned and said, "You need *this* pup at *this* time! This pup was born on April 12, *April 12*!" I couldn't respond. She stood there looking at me and said, "That's right, Easter Sunday, *Easter Sunday!* So on June 13, 1998, I traveled to Long Island, New York and picked up Sallie Mo, a Bichon puppy who was born on the third day after Good Friday, the day 'Sweet Mom' died. I should note that neither of us considered this a mystical re-birth of Mercedes, but rather a matter of symbolism of a timely birth, and the continuity and rejuvenation of life, perhaps even my own. Not only did I return with Sallie, but her mom also took the ride with us. She became known as Callie Lu, and now there were six.

September 1998, five months after Mercedes died and four months after Little Girl had left, Jock the start of it all, the patriarch, joined Pug, Mercedes, and Little Girl. At almost eighteen, his kidneys just quit. Anyone who has seen a dog battle kidney disease knows what an awful demise it is. Within five months, three had left me and I hoped that our family did not suffer losses for many years to come.

By the turn of the millennium, Portia and Brutus were getting on in years. Portia, like her father Jock, had cataract surgery years ago, but by now had lost most of her vision. Brutus, like his mom, remained free from that affliction, but he was slowing down. Both were finding it more and more difficult to negotiate the fourteen steps necessary to access our house over-looking the expansive views of the Albemarle Sound. So I decided to move. I rationalized the move to other humans, who decried my decision to leave such a desirable place, by claiming that several violent storms moving across the forty-mile expanse of open water caused the rebuild of three piers. Although I loved the boat trips with the dogs, and friends marveled at Norma Jean's jet-ski rides with Phoebe, I gave up the nautical life and moved to a one-story house with mostly ceramic tile floors instead of carpet. Ceramic tile allows for accidents and indiscretions brought about by old age and the two steps into the house provided easy access for geriatric Brutus, and blind Portia. Within two months after the new house was finished, Portia was diagnosed with a large, benign tumor on her liver. After she ate, the tumor forced her full stomach to press upon her vagus nerve stopping her heart and causing her to vomit while passed out. The unavoidable operation initially was a success, but it took its toll on my fifteen-year-old clown. Her health rapidly declined as she refused to eat. Her journey with me, which began at birth, lasted fifteen years and two months, and ended on Friday, July 13, 2001.

In November of 2002, Brutus left to join all the rest. He was the firstborn and the last to leave, noble and kind to the end. He died at the young age of sixteen years and six months. It is now 2007. As I sit at the kitchen table finishing this chapter, Little It, the ragged gremlin that appeared at my door in 1993, is over fifteen years old. Puppy, a rescue-dog from a hideous junkyard and hideous people came to me in 2004, badly malnourished, full of parasites, with a terribly matted coat besmeared with tar and grease, limping from a fishing line ingrown beneath the skin of his back leg, and containing ten abscessed teeth. He is resting calmly and contently (although mostly toothless) on the cool, tile floor. Sallie Mo and Callie Lu recline on their ever-present spot beside me on a specially concocted bench allowing for their preferred position.

I have tried to report this long history with dogs as succinctly as possible, only including the bare minimum of events, illustrating the arrival and the departure of my truest companions over a forty-four year journey. It is my background, but not my story. For as I have mentioned, to describe the journey each dog has taken me, with all the trappings, nuances of revelations, and concrete epiphanies would require volumes.

This book is not about my personal experiences with dogs. It is about your recognition and appreciation of the messages your dog reveals and the love he humbly offers. *It is about your journey, not mine.* Perhaps you think such an important topic should command more words, more pages with detailed dog dramas containing more philosophical observations. But like the dog, this book and the message it carries, is simple yet complex. It's a simple nudging to begin a journey: the path of which is multifaceted, the destination straightforward, and the reward compound.

This book is not a long one, and it doesn't need to be. Hopefully, the few simple words contained here will invite you to start *your* journey, leading you to add *your own story.* Then virtually, in that way, this book will become very long indeed.

Chapter 3

THE NON-KEEPERS

"We can judge the heart of a man by his treatment of animals."   Immanuel Kant

Many humans go through life having little contact with the noble dog and any incidental contact they may have is brief and superficial. Unfortunately, these humans deprive themselves interaction with this wonderful gift. With that said, I surely don't mean to imply that all humans should keep dogs. Unfortunately for the dogs, too many insensitive humans already do. Furthermore, many people briefly keep dogs because of an ill-timed, ill-fated decision made without understanding themselves or the dog. This group, on whim alone, hastily decides to keep a dog without any regard for the temperament of a breed and without considering even the basic responsibilities attached; and sooner than later, deem the dog a problem. Sometimes the *'problem'* dog is handed over to a more enlightened friend; or worse. Many times the unfortunate creature is taken to the closest pound and frequently exterminated. A fate destined to visit about three million of the species every year. It is not for these humans that this book is written. Unfortunately, they would fail to recognize the intent and the message would go unheeded. But to even these misguided people the dog presents a message: a plea for understanding.

To be sure, many humans have developed a negative opinion of the dog, even to the extent of harboring disdain usually brought about through fear. The media never fails to report episodes of a bicyclist mauled by a group of pit-fighters, or a little girl's face and body scarred by an attack of an Akita. As ridiculous and liberal as it may sound to some of you, these unfortunate acts of aggression are not the fault of the dog but rather the result of misuse and misdirection at the hands of human keepers. With his self-imposed, tenuous mastery, mankind purposely and selectively breeds valuable traits into existence and longevity, and when properly explored and responsibly utilized, benefit both man and dog. Discriminatory breeding for protective temperament and behavior benefits man's security of life and property. Selective breeding producing incredible scent abilities results in the rescue of many lost humans, saving them from certain death. And the selective process leads to the longevity of the herding breed, a necessity for livestock farmers, and a thing of wonder and beauty to behold at work. However, exploitation, misguided manipulation and misuse by a growing number of arrogant humans who, with reckless abandon, subvert the true nature of the dog. Man confuses the dog's once beneficial trait, polluting it by transference of fear and hate from within and instilling these into the unsuspecting nature of the dog whose only desire is to please his human keeper. Such is the nature of injudicious humans, not the true nature of any dog. For sure, the Bichon Frise has a different temperament from the Chow, but we humans have caused this to be so by our self-imposed mastery. So as we extol the virtues of the Border Collie so should we understand the character of the Pit Bull, realizing that using our free will to explore and cultivate our growth and development can result in beneficial results to all. But it can, if swayed by ego and fear, just as easily go awry, becoming convoluted, producing disastrous results, initiating our demise as well as the downfall of others. We tend to judge and condemn dogs on whom we force deviation from their true nature, rather than understanding and recognizing the culpability of *our* misguided manipulation and, in some drastic, disastrous cases, the true extent of *our* malicious shortcomings.

In ancient times, the function of the Chow was that of a first-line combatant against armed human opponents, and their aggression and courage was held in high esteem. But I have witnessed firsthand the love and gentleness exuded by this breed to their humans: humans who truly reciprocate and cultivate love instead of aggression. A particularly aggressive and unruly Chow visited a groomer friend of mine for a first-time bath and shave down. After many attempts to calm the dog, the groomer, a true dog lover, and a master at winning the trust of even the most aggressive dog clients, called the dog's human explaining the hopeless situation and requested that he pick up the dog. The man asked if he could come to the shop and try to calm the dog so the procedure could continue. After a short time, an older gentleman walked in and immediately knelt down beside the Chow and putting his face squarely on the dog's face, nose to nose, began whispering soft tones of love and affection while the groomer proceeded with the shave down. The man remained in this position gently whispering to his dog for twenty-five minutes while the shave down was completed without so much as a whimper out of the Chow. Such incidents reinforce the fact that mankind, despite efforts to ascribe his own aggressions and cruelty to the character of the dog, cannot extinguish the true goodness of the dog's soul. The soul of the dog is God's creation; and therefore cannot be truly conquered by mankind's hate and aggression. But the soul of the dog can be reached by love and through this love, love is returned. For it is not in the dog's world, if untampered with by humans, we find homicide, genocide, hatred, fear, and cruelty; but rather in our own.

When we judge the product of our manipulation, and more importantly our misuse of certain breeds, we must judge ourselves for the process, and the results. This, my friends, is part of the test of our development. As we trace the evolution of our relationship with dogs, so must we examine the development of our individual, and collective, spiritual character.

Chapter 4

EVOLUTION

When the Man waked up he said, 'What is Wild Dog doing here?' And the Woman said. 'His name is not Wild Dog any more, but the First Friend, because he will be our friend for always and always and always. Take him with you when you go hunting.'

Rudyard Kipling, from *"Just So Stories"*

Let's go back 140,000 years when our ancestor, the Homo sapiens, first appeared walking upright, emerged from his cave facing a forbidding, primeval world filled with many predators, more formidable than he, who were capable of having him for dinner. This is about the time when some scientists, like John Allman of the California Institute of Technology, in his book *Evolving Brains,* state that the partnership between wolves and humans was formed. Other scientists have evidence suggesting that around this time a partnership evolved into a bond between humans and *dogs*. It is interesting that research scientist Rupert Sheldrake, in his book *"Dogs That Know When Their Owners Are Coming Home",* points to DNA evidence indicating the first human-*dog* companionship occurred over 100,000 years ago.

"... recent evidence from the study of DNA and dogs and wolves points... to a date for the first transformation of wolf to dog over 100,000 years ago. This new evidence also suggests that wolves were domesticated several times, not just once and that dogs have continued to crossbreed with wild wolves...this theory...means that

ancient companionship with dogs may have played an important part in human evolution. Dogs could have played a major role in the advances of human hunting techniques that occurred some 70,000 to 90,000 years ago."

It was this domestication, the human-dog bond, which secured the survival of the frail Homo sapiens, around whom the early beneficial canines symbiotically congregated. Had this bond not occurred our ancestor could have faced the same extinction as his close cousin and competitor, the Neanderthal man. For no evidence exists which shows the Neanderthals or any other protohuman species now extinct, formed a mutually beneficial bond with canines.

So let's set the stage - 140,000 years ago. Humans (Homo sapiens) with their vegetarian like teeth, slow footed gait, faint sense of smell and hearing, unwieldy wooden clubs, and limited-range sticks with sharpened points, paled in comparison to the swift footed, collectively cunning, formidable hunting prowess of the canines. From a safe distance the small band of humans witness the canines tear into their prey and satisfy their hunger, after briefly squabbling among themselves just to establish hierarchy, the same way modern wolves do today. The wolves either moved on searching for the next prey or may have stayed with the present lunch, lounging around until time for dinner. Had the wolves moved on, the humans descended upon the kill and began their feast. If the pack remained, and if the human family was large enough, and most importantly hungry enough, they may have found the courage to charge the pack, driving them away temporarily.

So here we have set the scene. Either the pack of wolves had moved on by their own volition or the pack had been driven off. Either way the humans were satisfying their hunger on the backs of the canines. The pack who voluntarily abandoned the kill may have returned unsuccessful in finding a new quarry, or the pack driven off did not retreat far from the scene. In either case, the humans built a fire and set up camp, and were enjoying the fruits of the meal, with the canines menacingly roaming the periphery eyeing *their* kill. The apprehensive humans began to feel a little uncomfortable as the darkness of night approached and did what any survival-minded human would do: *they threw the dogs a bone!* Thus, the partnership was born and an everlasting bond was established. **Nowhere in history has this relationship ever been duplicated**.

What mysterious force caused the development of this plan: dogs helping humans survive in the harsh primitive world? Using the dog to help hunt and kill prey one hundred thousand years ago is an example of the earliest and most primeval interaction and man's wise use of the resources given to him. Evolution has altered the symbiotic relationship between man and dog, for no longer do we hunt prey with the help of dogs just to survive. Obviously, numerous examples of the symbiotic relationship between man and dog are well documented through the ages. However, from the earliest time the interaction began, man had to be awakened to the possibility before him. He had to recognize the dog as a resource. And over the years, it has been the most enlightened among us who accept the gift of the dog and the role he plays in our lives. A role illustrated by a myriad of examples. Witness the gratitude emanating from a rescued human lost and found in the remote regions of the snow-covered world by a dog. Observe the bond between a dog and the blind human he guides safely through a dark and perilous world. Pay attention to the joy on the faces of unfortunate, mentally handicapped children and adults as they experience stability and unconditional love while they hug a dog. Watch as loneliness is chased away from the room as a dog curls lovingly and acquiescently beside an ageing and infirmed patient in a nursing home. The list can go on and on. Many books study, illustrate, and document the benevolent role of dogs in our lives. In addition, the litany of contributions often defies explanation. Astounding accounts of dogs predicting epileptic seizures in humans; predicting earthquakes and tremors; predicting with uncanny accuracy when their owners will return home; and diagnosing with a high degree of accuracy the existence of cancer by smell have been scientifically documented, and theories have been advanced attempting to explain these phenomena. Yet they remain mysterious.

Certainly, much has been written about this noble creature and the role he plays in our lives. But this book travels a different path. Its premise is very simple. Dogs have a message for life and this message is one of hope and guidance. For at no time in our evolution do we need these messengers any more than we do now. With all the abundant choices between good and evil we have created for ourselves through our evolution, we have vastly complicated our relationship with ourselves, others, and God. A state of complication breeds confusion and a state of confusion can produce poor decisions.

At our disposal lay the abundant treasures of our corporeal world as well as the inherent riches of our individual soul. In simple terms, the question is begged: How will mankind use the physical and spiritual resources available to him? Will he use them wisely to his advantage as well as to the benefit of all creatures, or will he egotistically squander the resources and lose himself in the process? In the macrocosm (collective society) will we use our free will to decimate the physical and mental assets of society, or will we explore and cultivate them? In the microcosm, (individually) will we extol the resources given to our soul and use them for our own individual growth, or will we egocentrically squander them and destroy ourselves as the result? I know these are age-old questions, but are we evolving in the right way? We (collectively and individually) are free to choose our path, to decide our fate. Life is hard. Often we suffer not only because we make bad choices but also because life *is* hard. Suffering, hardship, and failures test our resolve and, if not properly dealt with, stunt our spiritual growth. Our spiritual survival is as tenuous today as our physical survival was when modern humans originated in Africa 140,000 years ago. It would be helpful if we had more Masters to guide us on our way. The good news is they do exist here with us. We only need to recognize them.

"Many Masters have been sent to the Earth to demonstrate Eternal Truth."

"These special messengers have been gifted with extraordinary insight, and the very special power to see and receive the Eternal Truth, plus the ability to communicate complex concepts in ways that can and will be understood by the masses."

"Conversations With God"

One-hundred thousand years ago, a mysterious force sent the dog to help us survive in a forbidding, primeval world. The trail of our evolution has led us from that primitive, dangerous world to where we are today, and to the *relative* physical safety and conveniences of our modern day existence. But in many ways, our survival is as tenuous and precarious as it was when man emerged from his cave. Now, as in times past, man has to recognize the dog as a messenger and teacher and must be able to open his heart and listen, truly listen. It is not about hunting prey for survival, but it *is* about survival. It is about the survival and growth of our collective and individual soul.

Chapter 5
EVOLUTION OF EGO - FREE WILL GONE AWRY

"Humankind has not woven the web of life. We are but one thread within it. Whatever we do to the web, we do to ourselves. All things are bound together. All things connect."

Chief Seattle

In the worldly scheme of things, humans believe we have been placed here as the master of our domain. The birds in the sky, fish in the sea, and all animals on earth exist to serve us. Given all this mastery, and believing we have been chosen for and appointed to this exalted position by God, our egos run wild. Disparate from all other creatures, we claim sole possession of a free will, being exclusively created in God's image. I can't think of a more presumptuous, more narcissistic, more egotistical conclusion.

The word creature is generally used to label, describe, and categorize all forms of life excluding ourselves. Humans would do well to climb down from their self-constructed, self-centered pedestal, for God hasn't given us tenuous mastery over other creatures, we have arbitrarily and undeservedly usurped it. It is emphatically sad but true that we have mastered the power to destroy most forms of life including ourselves. We have the ability to use this awesome power slowly or, since we have perfected technological techniques of destruction, we can accomplish obliteration in one grand finale. Whether we do it slowly, as we have been doing, without any regard for the consequences, or whether we do it in one fell swoop, is the question: the answer to be determined by our collective and individual free will.

What is this business about free will anyway and why is man the only creature on earth who possesses it? Much has been discussed, analyzed, and concluded about the two words 'free will'. Theologians, philosophers, psychiatrists and psychologists use this term to describe the divergence between us and all other creatures, commonly believing that because of 'free will' we are, among other things, at the top of the food chain, masters of all other creatures, and masters of ourselves; captains of our own ship so to speak. We tediously hang on to this theory believing, because God gave us free will, we are inherently the masters of our earthly domain. With our super-size egos intact, we proclaim, in thoughts, words, and deeds, ourselves to be gods on earth, master of all that is beneath us, and separated from all that is above us; demanding from all other creatures worship, praise, respect, and fear. Haughtily we separate ourselves from nature and God and thus violate another immutable law. But again, just what is free will? Simply put, free will is an option to choose a specific thought, word, or deed over another. A choice most humans erroneously believe no other creature on earth possesses. I contend that all creatures have a God-given free will. A free will that is demonstrated and implemented consistently within the boundaries of God's natural and universal laws, except by man. What separates humans from other creatures is not our exclusive right to free will but rather our inclination to transcend or ignore the immutable truths. All other creatures, exercising their free will, could elect to ignore these truths yet they do not, instinctively knowing transgression would eventually lead to their demise.

Supercilious man is the only creature with the temerity to challenge these laws and thus flirt with destruction. This boldness found roots in the early days of man's evolution. Since the moment man first found shelter in a cave, found a way to stay warm, and a way to satisfy hunger, his existence was rather tenuous. This frail creature encountered a world that was in no way kind to his slow-footed gait, poorly insulated covering, small vegetarian like teeth, poor sense of smell, faint sense of hearing, and his small, limited pupils that, at best, could discern *only shadows of things that go bump in the night*. How fearful this ill-suited specimen must have felt as he watched from his cave other creatures, more suitably equipped, easily survive the cold; and, witnessed creatures, more formidable in stature, proficiently kill prey to satisfy hunger. But early man, to his credit and mostly to our reward, compensated for his frailties by intelligence and cunning, and learned to survive. With his survival, he developed into a formidable hunter, a maker of tools, a builder of fire, and an engineer of societies. At that point, with his foothold of existence secured and his survival apparent, he shook his fist at nature, shouting to the heavens that no longer could nature defeat him. His temerity became bravery as he proclaimed himself master of his domain. A will to survive became a free will to conquer. Having survived and flourished *in* the natural world, now he could exist *outside* it, and the ego of the conqueror was at hand. With this spirit of conquest, mastery is proclaimed. And with this self-edifying proclamation, the immutable universal laws of nature are whimsically subverted and subdued. This practice, founded in the early days of man's evolution, prosecuted through the millennia, and superlatively perfected in modern times, sails our ship into dangerous waters. Humans should be very careful, very careful indeed; for to proclaim ourselves masters over the universal truths is luridly destructive and is not the same as *mastering* the principles of the truths. History has witnessed and chronicled the lives of wise and enlightened men, such as Jesus, Buddha, and Gandhi, who were masters of the universal truths. Theirs was the mastery of completely knowing, heeding and living by the immutable principles, operating and living within, *not outside*, them. A simple comparison: a master electrician knows and uses the principles of electricity to his benefit. He also knows that to ignore or subvert these principles is potentially very dangerous, indeed.

Many years have passed since our ancestor shook his fist at the primeval world in triumph of his survival. Since then, history has witnessed innumerable, momentous strides in the marathon of our evolution. Fertilized by our success, our egos have grown exponentially to immense and dangerous proportions. Considering ourselves supreme masters over the earth, we remain isolated, as pretentious masters are, from all that is below and above us. It is certainly true that over the last 140,000 years humans have been the impetus and the benefactors of evolution's advancements. Just the mere listing of the vast litany would fill volumes. Briefly, man has emerged from the cultures and democracies of Greece and the engineering wonders of the empire of Rome, to become the conqueror of the seas, architects of the earth and explorers of the heavens. The science of medicine just in the last few hundred years has evolved from bloodletting to cure headaches to the cloning and fertilization of embryos. We have found the causes and cures for many diseases and plagues. No longer do we communicate through rudimentary, guttural grunts and groans, but rather use cyberspace as a medium for our communications. However, with every progression of our culture since the dawn of man, our egos have grown, and along the way and at every point in our history the three letter word, ego, has been at the root of our collective cruelty to one another and has woefully stunted the spiritual growth of humanity.

Despite our great accomplishments, we now find ourselves standing on a precarious precipice. You may doubt such an ominous statement, recognizing that each and every generation going back to the dawn of man has heard harbingers of doom, soothsayers predicting the untenable continued existence of mankind. The Old Testament describes the story of the flood, the New Testament has the Book of Revelations, and each society and every era has its predictors and prognosticators of doom. In the fourteenth century, the Black Plague, believed sent by an angry God to eradicate mankind, destroyed over a third of the world's known population. But yet we survive.

One can argue that the human race has survived, evolved, and flourished despite many cataclysmic events. And short of an asteroid the size of Manhattan striking the earth, probably will survive many more. Nevertheless, our world has been bombarded by hideous, self-wrought injustices and cruelty, from which humanity narrowly escaped destruction. In the last sixty years alone, we witnessed World War II in which twenty million Russian troops, several million German and Japanese, and five-hundred thousand of our own brave men were killed; as well as the systematic murder of six million Jews in the killing centers of Hitler's concentration camps. As a final end to the deadly conflict, we saw the atomic obliteration of two cities in Japan, and as a result endured the imminent threat of nuclear, world annihilation during the Cold War. *Just to mention a few.*

Our city societies survive daily and numerous murders resultant from greed, anger, cruelty, and hate. With every inscrutable act of death wrought by self proclaimed saviors and cultists' like Charlie Manson and Jim Jones, and with the enigmatic, calculated murder of five young school girls in a benign Amish community, the health of our collective psyche is weakened. With every bloody encounter with religious terrorism, and with every prejudicial persecution of racial injustice, now or in hundreds of years past, our humanity diminishes and suffers. And with every rape and murder of a child, the moral fabric of society is violated and the innocence and goodness of our collective soul is either lost, or slowly but surely vanishing from view.

I struggle to resist my pessimistic opinion of humanity as I witness mankind's effort, or lack thereof, to progress toward a kinder, gentler nature. On our collective soul's path of evolution, we seem to be treading on a slippery slope, going nowhere. In fact, we are sliding dangerously backwards into an abyss of cruelty and callousness toward each other. Huckleberry Finn, whose wisdom and lack of ego completely overshadowed his lack of formal education, succinctly said it best when he regretfully observed that, "*Human beings can be awful cruel to one another.*" Huck, the epitome of nobility, was also a master of understatement!

How much longer can this cruelty last before it poisons the collective bloodstream of our humanity? What will it take to replace callousness with love and respect for each other? Perhaps looking up to the heavens asking for a second coming of a Savior - a teacher from above; or maybe, in the interim while waiting for this miracle, we need to look down at our feet discovering an eager teacher: the noble dog.

Chapter 6

WHAT IS A GREAT TEACHER ?

"There are many such teachers among you, as always there have been, for I will not leave you without those who would show you, teach you, guide you, and remind you of these truths."
"Conversations With God"

I came out of college young and dumb. Sure, I had gone through the curriculum prescribed by the state, passed with flying colors the college courses required, even did well on the national teacher's exam. But even though my college bestowed upon me a degree and the State of Virginia granted a license to teach at the secondary level, I wasn't, by any stretch of the imagination, a teacher. But in my young exuberance and naïveté, I was convinced of my abilities. I resigned as a teacher after one year. That's been over thirty-four years ago. In the past years I have learned and digested some hard lessons presented by harsh, malevolent teachers; useful lessons taught by good teachers; and sublime lessons demonstrated by great teachers.

Life as a Teacher

Life has been called a teacher of sorts - sometimes a very harsh one at that. It is often the very worst teacher we ever will have. Many of the lessons it brings serve to destroy our confidence, our will to achieve, and sometimes our will to survive. Life serves up a plateful of failures and disappointments. We don't have the option to choose whether we're going to eat or not, but we do have control over how the 'hard to swallow' servings affect our character. Life is not a compassionate teacher either, for it forces us to swallow all of its lessons good and bad. What we find within us, within our spirit, teaches us how to make the best out of life's failures and hardships. Contrastingly, a good teacher is one who helps us digest life's lessons, store them, and use them for the betterment of our mind and spirit. Life is not a fair teacher either; but a good teacher is one who gently nudges us to realize that not all things in life are fair and it only matters how we cope with life's unfairness.

A Great Teacher

A great teacher, unlike life, is not one who demands our attention. We give our attention because we realize his great wisdom and we listen because we will benefit. A great teacher doesn't slap us upside our head or crack our knuckles with a ruler to get our attention. He knows that causing pain in this manner will only serve to divert our attention, not attract it. His technique is one of subtlety. He delivers his lessons with calmness and grace. The magnetism by which he attracts us to his truth is clarity and selflessness. A great teacher rejoices in our progress and is overjoyed by it. He teaches not for his betterment or ego, but rather for our self-improvement. He loves us not only for what we are, but also for what he knows we can become. He knows the spiritual potential we all possess, and is confident of the grace we all are capable of reaching. Gently, but unremittingly, he nudges us toward the awareness of both.

The deeds and actions of a great teacher are inextricable from his lessons and character, and his nobility and integrity are the vehicles for the lessons of life. He practices what he teaches. He is persuasive and patient. He is aware, that being human, our frail minds can often stray as our attention fails, but undaunted by our shortcomings in this regard, he gently herds our thoughts back into the fold and starts the lesson over again.

The lessons of a great teacher are simple and simplistic in context and deliverance. His concepts are not clouded with compound, complex run-on sentences replete with esoteric words or phrases. Some of our philosophers/ teachers make a habit of confusing their students with complexities of style and text, but the style of the great teacher is simple and his lessons are universal, applying to all humanity, not just the occult few. His lessons speak to all men in all tongues and languages. His teachings and lessons are not convoluted or stymied by language, and it is not the eloquence of language that transmits the message; it is the element of love. And a great teacher is the personification of unconditional love. There have been many *near great* teachers who have walked this earth. Socrates, Gandhi, Buddha, Mother Teresa, Martin Luther King, and Albert Schweitzer are but a few on the list. Although their teachings and lessons are invaluable to humanity and their lives a near model for us to emulate, they were human. As with all humans, flaws of character are simply a fact of life. Granted, the near great teachers mentioned had far less foibles than the vast majority of us, but they still had a personal agenda, which included the quest for self-enrichment, not monetary enrichment, but rather personal satisfaction and, to some slight degree, the acclaim of others. A great teacher stands in stark contrast to the near great in this, and therein we find the most important distinction between the two. The great teacher is willing to forgo all of this world's comforts and rewards, considers accolades inconsequential, and is willing to sacrifice his whole being to teach the great lessons of humility, forgiveness, tolerance, loyalty, love, truth, and joy.

By now, I guess you have determined there is only one in all of history that reaches the status of a great teacher, and your conclusion is correct. There is however one caveat to this conclusion: the dog. I can feel your skepticism jumping from these pages slapping me squarely between my eyes. How dare I mention Jesus and the dog in the same sentence or even inviting a comparison? But, bear with me. Jesus walked on earth to offer the joy of salvation, teach the ultimate truth, and demonstrate unconditional love. For two-thousand years, we have heard the promise of the second coming to strengthen our faith. In the meantime, we have at our disposal a noble, selfless, patient, and loving teacher: the ubiquitous dog. The dog holds within the simple yet great truths of the universe and his purpose is to deliver the messages in a sublime yet simple way, with a truth and clarity that men of all languages can understand. To be sure, the great truths of the universe transcend contrivances and idiosyncrasies of language. In fact, they need not to be verbalized at all, and are best taught by demonstration. Suzanne Clothier, in her insightful book, *"If A Dog's Prayers Were Answered Bones Would Rain From the Sky"*, eloquently illustrates this concept:

"We proudly claim language is that which sets us apart from (dogs), and yet when language fails us as it often does in the face of profoundly moving experiences, the… quality of pure gesture is all that we have left. To my way of thinking, it is not a sad commentary… that they do not have verbal or written language by which to express their feelings, be that love, or sympathy or joy or grief. It is, I think, a rather telling note that when we are most deeply moved, we return to the pure eloquence of communication that they use all along. We are, sometimes, most eloquent when we are dumb."

What better vehicle to transmit these messages than the dog, whose language, because they are dumb, is action and deeds, and therefore universal. Their non-verbal monologue delivers the sublime, universal truths as they demonstrate a steadfast, unconditional love as true as can be experienced in our physical world.

Perhaps you are still skeptical about this proposition, but as you finish this book, I am positive you will see the connection. Just listen.

Chapter 7

LISTENING

"*How does God talk, and to whom? When I asked this question, here's the answer I received:*"

"I talk to everyone. All the time. The question is not to whom I talk, but who listens?"

You just read an excerpt from Neale Walsch's book, "*Conversations with God*". What if you *could* talk to God? If you had an opportunity to ask God questions, would you doubt the answers given and suspect the source? Would you be skeptical if a great prophet and spiritual teacher appeared before our society?

I suspect that some would listen and some would turn a deaf ear, but the vast majority would remain incredulous and with valid reasons. David Koresh, Jim Jones, and Charles Manson are three deadly reasons for our incredulity. Other individuals such as Ted Haggard, Jimmy Swaggert, and Jim and Tammy Bakker simply were exposed as hypocrites and frauds, which is serious enough to followers who succumbed to their doctrine. No wonder our skepticism tends to question the motives of self-proclaimed saviors and prophets, and others who claim to have a direct line of communication with the Almighty. In the wake of false prophets, we find ourselves floating on the sea of incredulity and skepticism. The fear of being duped causes many of us to turn a deaf ear to those who claim to know firsthand the spirit of God and the truths of the universe.

Attributed to this fear is the disparagement and persecution of those who were genuine. Mahatma Gandhi devoted his life to changing the injustices and the inequalities of this world through peaceful action and love, and for that, he was assassinated by jealousy and hate. Martin Luther King, who devoted his life to a vision and dream of racial equality and peace among men, lost his life to a bullet fired by ego and fear. Two thousand years ago, society crucified a Savior, a 'son of man' and the Son of God. For two millennia, some have listened to the words of Jesus, but to the virtual majority the teachings of the Master have fallen on either deaf or cynical ears.

How many of us adore and attempt to emulate every action, hang on every word spoken and every thought expressed by our individual and collective idols? How many of our teenagers swoon over and feverishly emulate the appearance and the actions of Brittany Spears, or the myriad of rap artists. If the teens, or the rest of us glued to *breaking news*, would truly listen to the thoughts, words and actions of their idols without succumbing to worship in the physical sense of the relative world, they would realize the folly of their adulation. Nevertheless, all of us are limited by the nearsightedness of the physical and relative world, and unfortunately, we aspire to emulate and strain to listen to the ephemeral, dubious heroes to whom we are devoted. Little by little, day by day the character of a society is changed by the desire to emulate the traits of famous or infamous *people* it admires, regardless of their quality. This is true when our individual evolution is in its infancy, regardless of our chronological age. And it is a necessary progression as well as a universal truth, and here's why.

The world of the relative, the world of false reality, or the world of the physical, however you want to label it, must be experienced in order to grow spiritually and to aspire to the world of the absolute, the realm of our soul. It is within the realm of the soul where we experience the 'oneness with the universe', and where we find the 'mystical union'. It is not my intent here to offer a treatise on Mysticism but a brief mention is necessary to understand the role of the dog in our quest to be in touch with our soul and leave behind the illusion of reality contained in the relative or physical world, with its landscape of fear, hate, and ego. For as we enter, regardless of how briefly, the spiritual realm of our soul - the world of the absolute - we leave behind the relative world and it's discordant cacophony of false noises by which our hearing and listening is impaired and muted. Only then can we begin to hear the harmony and the clarity in the universal expressions: love, truth, and joy. Our journey through the relative world and our emergence from it is a necessary one. Fear, hate, and ego and the suffering they cause must be experienced before they can be transcended. The journey to the realm of the soul must pass through the hardships and pitfalls of the false reality of the physical world.

On our journey from the relative world to the realm of our soul, we are fortunate to have a helmsman: a creature with whom a bond was formed thousands of years ago. And, who by his own volition, because of his love, joins the human's relative world as a guide. A visitor who, in thoughts and expression, still belongs to the world of the absolute, the world of nature, the realm of the soul (his as well as ours) where God inextricably exists. Certainly, this is where we find God; for by His nature and true spirit, He cannot exist in the relative world of negativity, ego, fear, and hate. You may think the proposition of a dog as a spirit guide is a little far fetched. But try keeping an open mind and know this to be true: God created *all* creatures including man and all are, in and of themselves, inherently part of His spirit, and He is innately part of all souls. The collective soul of nature, of which dogs are a part, is not alienated from God, and *nor is the human soul*. It is our physical side, the part that shook its fist at nature years ago, that lives a life removed. And remember this: The creation, human or non-human, cannot be truly or permanently separated from the Creator, from and by whom both were equally created, and to Whom all creations, in their perfection, must return. What creature is more capable of guiding us around the pitfalls of our relative world, *re-introducing* us to our soul, and reuniting us with our Creator than the dog: the antithesis of hate, ego, and negativity, and the epitome of love, truth, and joy?

Perhaps you remain skeptical of the role and importance of the lowly, ubiquitous dog in such a momentous endeavor of leading us to unite in thought and word with the Creator. Many would consider this proposition anthropomorphic and ridiculous, believing such a task best left to the theologians, clergymen, and their religion. I might be inclined to agree if the counselors of man-made religions would stop portraying themselves as sole, preeminent interpreters, and in some cases the originators, of God's words and teachings. With that said, I ask you to stop and consider for few moments how out of touch the dogmas and doctrines of the religious chosen few are and have been. They teach that infants at birth are tainted with sin - Original Sin: a sin reportedly caused by someone else long-ago which precludes the contaminated from seeing or reuniting with God should they die prior to having this infraction removed by some special human. If I remember the Bible correctly, wasn't it Jesus who said, *"Let the little children come unto me"*, and then He blessed them? We are taught that the evil realm of hell and its presiding figure actually exist somewhere in the world of an omnipresent God because of a feud - a battle instigated by some uprising, discontent angels against the Almighty. Are we really to believe that the omnipotent Creator of the universe, the one Who always was and always will Be, allowed this battle, and the subsequent creation of hell and its curator, to occur?

Now, does my anthropomorphic proposition sound so ridiculous?

When we are very young, our religious mentors teach us that followers of any religion other than our own will never see the 'Kingdom of Heaven'. Some religions even teach that the 'Kingdom' will contain only a predetermined number of the chosen. Because of such dogmas, many horrific wars have been and will continue to be waged and many warriors have died and will die with the name of their god on their lips. Twenty-nine hundred people died by the hand of religious fanaticism on 9/11, and, right or wrong, the crusades begin again. How many heads rolled from the gallows built by man's religious intolerance demonstrated by moral cleansings such as the Spanish Inquisition? How many so-called witches burned at pyres, or died hanged at the gallows built at the altar of puritanical superstition and fear? Religious pundits placed Galileo under house arrest when he dared to publish his discovery establishing the sun as the center of the solar system, releasing him only after he reluctantly recanted his theory. During the Roman Inquisition, so-called heretics were executed, placed in a boiling mixture of oil, tar, and turpentine just for reading a Bible written in a language other than Latin. We have been reminded for years by bombastic, fire and brimstone preachers that God is an angry, vindictive Creator willing to obliterate his own creations. Hell, it used to be a sin to eat meat on Friday. Such are the treacherously dangerous and ridiculous teachings and dogmas of man, not God. With all this in mind, examine the words, thoughts, and deeds of the religious dogma of man and put them to this test: do their teachings, words, thoughts and deeds follow the example of the 'Master', truly containing and demonstrating love, truth, and joy?

Now consider the dog. Which of the two, the pretentious pundits or the unassuming dog, is the true purveyors of the Highest thought - joy, the Highest word or expression - truth, or the Grandest feeling - love? To be sure, neither man nor dog created these terms, but the dog, not man, personifies them. So I ask, isn't it about time that we give credibility and esteem to a messenger who, by example, brings into our lives joy, truth and love, rather than listening to the opinion of a dictatorial, self-appointed pundit who presents a perversely fearful and hatefully egotistical interpretation of the terms?

So if we would quiet the noises and ignore the attractions of the physical world; if we allow our egos to be stilled, and let ourselves be nudged toward love, truth, and joy by the dog's quiet soul; and, if we follow him and connect with the Center of our spirit, then each and every one of us might be able to talk with God. Then who among us could - or would - refuse to listen?

Chapter 8

FROM LISTENING…TO LOVE

"The first duty of love is to listen."   Paul Tillich

It is sad but true that we teach our kids to read adequately well, write a little, and listen less. This is so because teachers and parents, concentrating their efforts on subjects they deem important, leave the art of listening out of the curriculum altogether. So much so, that listening is rapidly becoming a lost art to all. This is a disturbing commentary on our society for it is our own self-centeredness, egotism, and narcissism that hinder the act of listening, making its instruction even more indispensable. Even though our eardrums reverberate to the waves of sounds, we just don't take them in. The sounds just don't register.

Failure to listen is truly a great character flaw of the human species and is one of the most glaring, unfortunate distinctions between us and the *rest* of the animal world. How long would the quail last in the bush if he didn't hear the coming of the fox? Of course, as the self-appointed masters of our world, we have abandoned the need to listen to the messages, pleasant or ominous, of the world around us. Sadly, not only have we abandoned listening to insure our survival, we have abandoned listening to others, human and non-human, and essentially have lost our love for them. Our self-absorbed nature is such that we concentrate selfishly on our past, present, and future; however, listening to another requires our undivided attention to the speaker in the present. Unlike dogs, creatures completely grounded in the present, we humans constantly muddle our minds, confusingly interweaving the events of our past with the worry or anticipation over our future. Thus, we miserably fail to pay attention. It's not that we have lost the ability to listen but, because of our self-centeredness, we have lost the desire.

Why is it so that on our first date with our future lover we hang on every word spoken? We listen with all ears, we hang on every word so that our date will feel important and, thus, cared for. After the honeymoon is over, the listening part is put in the freezer with the top layer of the wedding cake. For the most part, we are poor listeners. We forget, or maybe completely never knew, that listening to another is the highest form of respect and love. We haven't lost the ability to listen; maybe we have just misplaced our manners, and lost our respect and love for one another.

In his book *"The Road Less Traveled"*, M. Scott Peck relates an insightful commentary on what it means to listen to another. He attended a lecture given by a famous expert concerning the relationship between psychology and religion. He relates the speaker was putting forth a tremendous effort trying to make his listeners understand the extremely abstract topic and concepts. After the lecture, Peck admitted he didn't grasp any more than fifty-percent of what the speaker said and he felt completely drained and exhausted by his efforts to listen and understand every word spoken and every concept offered. Afterwards, while speaking to others who attended the lecture, he was amazed to hear that most were disappointed with the speaker saying he was incompetent and they learned absolutely nothing. Peck, unlike the others, got much more out of the lecture and he goes on to say why:

> "In contradistinction to the others, I was able to hear much of what this great man said, precisely because I was willing to do the work of listening to him. I was willing to do this work for two reasons: one, because I recognized his greatness and that what he had to say would likely be of great value; second, because of my interest in the field I deeply wanted to absorb what he had to say so as to enhance my own understanding and spiritual growth. My listening to him was an act of love. I loved him because I perceived him to be a person of great value worth attending to, and I loved myself because I was willing to work on behalf of my growth. Since he was the teacher and I pupil, he the giver and I the receiver, my love was primarily self-directed, motivated by what I could get out of the relationship and not what I could give him. Nonetheless, it is entirely possible that he could sense within his audience the intensity of my concentration, my attention, my love, and he may have been thereby rewarded. Love (and listening) as we shall see again and again, is invariably a two-way street, a reciprocal phenomenon whereby the receiver also gives and the giver also receives."

The quote from Peck's book illustrates the most prominent reason we should listen to another. To reiterate, "my listening to him was an act of love. I loved him because I perceived him to be… of great value, and I loved myself because I was willing to work on behalf of my growth". By God's intention, the dog is a teacher and messenger of 'great value' and we should listen to him on 'behalf of (our) growth'. But unlike Peck's lecturer, listening to the message of the dog is not hard work. It's *easy listening*. He communicates with universal language and in simple terms. Once you recognize your dog is a creature of great value and you learn to listen, then you will truly come to respect and love him, accepting him as your guide on the road of discovery: discovery of yourself and the awareness of spiritual growth.

And so it follows that if failure to listen to others is a result of our narrow-minded, self-absorbed nature, then the act of listening is a result of our willingness to extend our love and respect to another, whether it be a human or a dog. When we are truly listening, we are truly loving another. Since love and respect are emotions and emotions are grounded in the heart, it must be so that listening is done with the heart. And heart to heart, soul to soul is the only medium of communication that is infallible and, befittingly, the dog's only option. If we respond in kind, we truly begin to listen, learn, and most importantly, understand. And with understanding comes spiritual growth within.

Love is the vehicle by which the dog's message is delivered from his heart to yours. And, with your heart and with your love, as you listen, the grandeur, worth and spirituality of the dog become apparent.

Chapter 9
IN THE PRESENCE OF DOGS

"Dogs are our link to paradise. They don't know evil or jealousy or discontent. To sit with a dog on a hillside on a glorious afternoon is to be back in Eden, where doing nothing was not boring – it was peace."   Milan Kundera

In 1994, a survey of seventeen European countries along with Canada, Australia, and the United States was compiled showing the number of households that contained dogs. The United States was second on the list with thirty-eight percent of households keeping dogs. Eight countries registered in the thirty percentile, but one stood far ahead of the rest: Poland. In Poland fifty-percent of the households kept dogs. To my knowledge, no one has done a study explaining the relationship between the national character of a country and the husbandry of dogs. If I were not so lazy regarding pure science, and research is a science, I would be interested in finding out why Poland led the field by such a wide margin. But for now, I can only offer an interesting, although unscientific, guess. During World War II Poland, more than any country conquered and occupied by Nazi Germany, was the most devastated in population and infrastructure. If my memory serves me correctly, over two million Jews, about seventy-percent of the Jewish population in that country, were systematically and hideously exterminated. In the aftermath of such cruel devastation, perhaps the children who survived, reaching the age of fifty or sixty in 1994, having seen the evilness and cruelty of such carnage manifested by murder and destruction, needed some kind of touchstone with, and semblance of, love and kindness. To fulfill this need, perhaps these children of war found the ubiquitous dog and instilled the love and veneration for this companionship in their children as well.

During our history as a nation, we are fortunate to have escaped such destruction to our country and our people. Nevertheless, evil, cruelty, and misery pervade our society. Racial and religious prejudice still exist in more minds and hearts than most will admit. Senseless acts of cruelty and hatred affect our condition of humanity nationally and globally. Almost daily, the nightly news reports the abduction, rape, and murder of a young child. Senseless waste of human life over the distribution of mind-altering substances is a daily part of the newscast entering our homes. Headlines describe corporate greed beyond imagination ruining the lives and futures of unsuspecting believers in a just and fair system. All too often, television airwaves resound with the sound of gunshots fired by troubled young students who turn institutions of learning into houses of death. And we witness, via live television broadcasts, the murder of thousands at the cold hand of terrorism. Most of us are fortunate that we have been spared firsthand experience of such events, but we all know that things happening in someone else's backyard could one day show up at our front door. This may explain why the latest data shows that forty-four percent of the households in this country keep dogs. By 1996, there were fifty-three million dogs in the United States. And, according to the latest census done in 2007, that number has increased to seventy-four million. Perhaps some keep dogs to provide physical protection, but I think the majority are kept to protect the condition of our psyche.

If you remember, as stated in the Chapter 4, 'Evolution', part of the test is man's wise use of the gift and resources made available to him, the dog being one of the most important of these gifts. As stated, it has only been the most enlightened humans who have recognized and made wise use of these gifts throughout the ages. Most humans are destined to fail this test by either not recognizing the resource or by misusing it. There are those who keep dogs in a beneficial but strictly secular and pragmatic relationship *without* recognizing and exploring the divine bond. Then, there are those humans who keep dogs for the mutual destruction of themselves and others, including the dog. And, there are many who really don't know why they keep them at all. These are the three stages where most humans are gathered: these are the 'keepers' of dogs; and, ironically, the three gradations of the **'keepers of God'**.

My purpose in this book isn't to chide or belittle anyone who finds himself in these stages of development. If I were to scold or ridicule I would be at total odds with the method and lessons of the Great Teacher and his messenger: the dog. To be sure, I am not the messenger and I don't pretend to have the gifts within me. My intent is to give the reader information and insight based on my personal experience and, by that experience, to urge the reader toward *awareness* of the dog as a gift and a guide to spiritual growth. I have been through the stages and to my detriment aimlessly lingered longer than necessary, misguided by lack of awareness. My intent here, like the dog, is to nudge you gently to this awareness.

Chapter 10
STAGES OF AWARENESS - THE KEEPERS

"He is your friend, your partner, your defender, your dog. You are his life, his love. He will be yours, faithful and true, to the last beat of his heart. You owe it to him to be worthy of such devotion."
Anonymous

The Misdirected

First, let's look at the misdirected. The guy lives four-doors down the street with his girlfriend and two Rottweilers. He is a recluse of sorts never inviting anyone to his home, disdaining most all human contact, except the bare necessities. One never gets to know him for he is known only by his laconic conversations, talking only in general and impersonal phrases, except when he relates stories about how his oldest and most obedient dog performs in school. "He is a trained attack dog, ready at my command to rip up any person to protect my property and me". As I stand on the side of the street listening, I maintain a safe distance from the mammoth head of the Rottweiler peering disdainfully and ominously at me out of the back window of the SUV. "Yep, he is a real mean-ass dog alright, bad to the bone to everyone except me and my girlfriend and he knows better than to come at me. I'll beat the crap out of him". That Rottweiler, just like any Toy Poodle, was not born to this disposition; this is not his intended gift. No doubt, many humans do keep dogs for protection, and for many years have trained and used them to protect livestock, property, and family. And this is a noble job. Many humans love and cherish their dogs for the performance of this job while recognizing the gifts dogs demonstrate. But judging from the harsh commands and his threatening tone of voice, no such love was indicated by this man to his Rottweiler. The dog, a natural protector of the humans he loves, will unselfishly give his own life to protect and serve. Because of his *love,* he performs honestly and faithfully. But somebody is missing the point in the relationship between this keeper and the dog. Someone is missing the point all right and that someone isn't the dog. This human has misdirected and misunderstood the gift and message of this dog. Because of his gift of love, the dog's performance of a duty comes naturally to him and demonstrates his expression of the gift. However, to singularly train and concentrate on aggressive behavior, extolling its virtue and considering it the ultimate function, misinterprets the whole point and fails to appreciate the benefit and resource. It is as misdirected as only using the gift of fire to commit arson.

The Oblivious

The misdirected, as seen above, is also oblivious, oblivious to the essence of the dog as a teacher. However, the oblivious keeper is only just that - oblivious. He does not keep the dog to satisfy his ego of being 'macho-master', reveling in the prowess of his dog as a killer while masking his own lack of courage. The oblivious doesn't really know why he has a dog; he is simply and only *unaware*. There may have been a reason why he obtained a dog in the first place but that reason has long since been forgotten; or perhaps the dog's presence is just a product of whimsical decision made by an oblivious mind. He merely goes through his daily motions of living or maybe just existing since his wife and the kids left three months ago. He rises in the morning, readies for work and as part of his morning routine makes a perfunctory trip to the doghouse to see if the dog has enough water to last the day and to make sure he remains attached to the chain that shackles him to the tree. The black and brown, small, mixed-breed dog, seeing his human, bounds out of the doghouse. The chain jingles around his neck as he shakes off the cold of the night; and with that accomplished, his whole body begins twisting and turning, with tail frantically wagging, in an effort simply to say 'good morning'. Through eyes crusted with sleep and dirt, his unrequited love and devotion showers this man walking from the house. The human stands over the water bowl and seeing the green slime in the bottom vows to provide freshwater when he returns home from work. He notices the flies hovering around the food dish and thinks he should clean it someday before depositing more of the same commercial slop he had dispensed into it a couple of nights ago. He stands just beyond the chain's reach and slightly and inadvertently pats the dog on the head. The dog wanting to contact his object of devotion attempts to offer muddy paws as a greeting, shouting 'Hello, I have missed you'. The human mumbles something like 'get down,' and turns and walks away. Straining against the chain the dog stretches forward in an effort to say, 'stay a minute, listen to me for a time. I love you'. Throwing his body against the chain, he stands on his hind legs, his muddy paws feverishly and futilely scratching at the air. The human quickly enters the house and without glancing back hurriedly goes about his business of life. He is oblivious to the love that was before him: a love offered completely and with no conditions. A love that is so absolute and compelling that no amount of dirt on his unkempt coat or mud on his paws can disguise. Despite his outward appearance, he loves with a clean heart and while his show of love can be constrained by the physical confines of the heavy rusted chain around his neck, there are no chains around his heart.

A block away lives another dog, a Golden Retriever, whose neglect is just as obvious. Although he resides in a warm house at night, is an occasional victim to the odious pain of a cleansing at the hands of a groomer, and possesses wonderful possible play toys - kids, the humans in this household are no more responsive to his gesture of love than the last human depicted, and are just as oblivious. This dog was a Christmas *toy* placed under the tree a few years ago and now, like most toys, no longer captures interest. In addition to feeding the dog, and keeping him clean, these humans have taught the dog all sorts of acceptable manners, evoking admiration by other, outside humans who enter this domain and lavish praise upon these humans for their good care offered to the dog, considering them good dog '*owners*'. Moreover, when they drop off the dog at the Vets for two weeks every year while they go on vacation, these humans always specify the bombardment of vaccines be administered, and a bath be given. These humans are doing their social best to keep up appearances and acceptability.

The Chance

The circumstances of the Rottweiler, the black and brown mix, and that of this Golden Retriever, although somewhat different, are very much the same. Each has been afforded the same opportunities to teach its lessons: slim to none. But slim is somewhat of a chance after all. One day, for some reason, the humans in the pictures provided might abandon their self-centeredness and listen to the message that each dog strains at the end of his chain to deliver. One night, while doing battle with an ominous intruder intent on harming his human, the Rottweiler is critically injured. As he lays suffering from his wounds after vanquishing his foe, pure goodness and selflessness of his soul emanates from his eyes reaching out to his human. His courage and devotion touch even this cold, egotistical, and cowardly heart. And the human begins to listen.

On a bitterly cold night as he breaks the ice formed on the water bowl and dumps the cold mush on to the filthy plate, the human looks into the eyes of the black and brown mix for the first time. These eyes are saying, "I will be alright out here in this miserable cold, for this is not the first time, and I have become used to it. But look into my soul and see my love for you. My love will keep you warm and comfortable, and I will ease your fears on this dreadful lonely night. If only you would talk with me for a time, I'll warm your soul and chase away the loneliness with my love". For the first time, this human looks into the eyes of this dog, removes the chain and together they walk inside the house. Sitting down in his favorite chair the human lets his arm dangle over the side to the area where the dog patiently sits. Slowly and gently, the dog nudges the hand with a cold, wet nose and touches the human's lonely heart with warm, unconditional love. The human begins to listen.

The youngest child in the socially correct household returns from school after just another day of suffering the 'slings and arrows' of his peers. He is a slight child, a kindhearted, meek youngster, quiet and shy. His glasses have been broken this day. He has been the object of teasing and ridicule that escalated into a physical catastrophe. As he enters the house, he feels his loneliness. His mother will not be home from work for another two hours and she will be in a frantic hurry to prepare the nightly meal for a preoccupied father. His brother and sister will only tease about his troubles when they arrive about the same time. He enters his room and sits quietly on the floor sobbing and wondering why he is so disliked. The tears of pain and loneliness blur his eyes. Quietly, without warning, the Golden Retriever appears. The boy can only see a blur as the dog gently but deliberately licks the tears from the child's face. Instinctively and for the first time, the boy reaches out for his only friend in life and places his arms around the strong and noble neck of this dog who is now more deliberately licking away the tears. A bond is forever formed with the only creature in his world that refuses to judge and offers to love. And the youngster begins to listen.

The Hope

A ray of hope is offered to the keeper of pit fighters - Pit Bulls. We haven't seen this human yet but we know about reports of his tools and his trade. In a remote region of the countryside he has thrown an abducted Sheltie into the pit as practice for his prize champion. The big fight is tonight and his undefeated champion must be in top form to meet his next formidable foe. So, in goes the quivering Sheltie. The human watches as his champion lunges for the death grip and finding it lays open the throat in one swift move. A steel vice of teeth clamps relentlessly squeezing the last heartbeat of life from the sacrificed victim. A gushing pulsating river of red pours from the Sheltie's neck soaking into the yellow sawdust. As the pit-fighter nudges his lifeless prey as if to make sure the job is complete, the human speaks of the great training and the prowess of his champion and remarks, "I have bred him to be the best but my training and hard work has really made him a champion." That night in the ring at the great fight, this champion meets a greater one. As he lay dying, his human trainer and admirer kneels beside him as he takes his last breath. The champion's neck has been

71

laid open and the bright red blood of life stains the sawdust floor. The eyes of the dying champion no longer flash the evil maliciousness instilled in him so expertly by his trainer. As the vanquished champion lay dying, the trainer's evil has lost its grip, replaced by the natural goodness of the dog's soul. For the first time in his career as a keeper and trainer of pit-fighters, and indeed for the first time in his life, the human looks into the soul of a champion and sees love in the eyes of a dog. And he begins to listen.

*Author's note: The writing of this book was completed just weeks before the alleged connection with Michael Vick and the hideous practice of dog fighting. Hopefully, as the evidence and the facts of this case are brought to light, so will the cruelty of the so called 'sport' of dog fighting be exposed to the mainstream public, as will the gruesome and revolting nature of its human participants.

Chapter 11

STAGES … AND BEYOND

*"The gift which I am sending you is called a dog, and is in
fact the most precious and valuable gift to mankind."*
                                        Theodorus Gaza

Sadly, the representations of the first three scenes
are performed and observed on numerous stages in every
community throughout the land. Although the fourth scene
is less frequently practiced, and less frequently observed, it
is more prevalent than many of us think. A cloud of secrecy
looms around the pit-fighters, but this hideous, covert cult
nevertheless pervades the country. The four examples
presented above are authentic, unromanticized testaments
to the waste of the dog as a gift and a resource. In an
attempt to overshadow the reality of the waste and provide
a ray of hope, the sudden, dynamic changes of the human's
heart depicted are somewhat optimistic. Each of the scenes
provides hope for human enlightenment, but seldom do
such dramatic epiphanies result in a complete revision of the
human's point-of-view. In fact, most human enlightenment
does not occur so simply and concisely. Because of our self-
centered nature and our busy lifestyle of self-absorption,
we seldom recognize the goodness of the dog except in bits
and pieces: little slices of the lessons. These slices are pieces
of an incomplete puzzle and are tiny, nebulous black-and-
white snapshots of the panoramic and technicolor picture.
The indelible snapshots are filed away in the archives of our

minds until someday, mysteriously and serendipitously, all of the slices meld together and the true worth of the gift is recognized. Then and only then, can we begin to focus in on the rainbow leading to the destiny of our journey. To be sure, my personal journey began at the young age and at a point in time when I was only able to experience bits and pieces - 'snapshots' which I stored away in my file cabinet of life. It took many of these messengers finally to nudge me into collating the bits and pieces into the final development of the panoramic view, and I still have a long journey ahead to appreciate it completely. In fact, I am proud to admit that converting thoughts to printed words contained in this book compelled a deeper appreciation for the dog as well as further progression along my path, another testament to the dog's enduring mission achieved by patient and persistent nudging.

The dog is a patient teacher and by his intuition he knows that seldom, if ever, his singular presentation will start the 'ball rolling' and conquer our heart in one fell swoop. But his gentle tenacity to deliver his message is ever present and never falters. So intense is his purpose and diligence in the performance of the mission, he contently provides even the 'negative' of the snapshots used in the menagerie of awareness. If his human is at a point in life where a snapshot is all his pupil can accept, so be it. The snapshot of love in the eyes of the dying pit-fighter; the snapshot of the noble, non-judging Golden; and the snapshot of the comforting nose of the 'black and brown mix' guarding against the cold loneliness of the night are slices of the lessons patiently offered over and over again. Offered by either the same messenger, or repeated by the ones who follow. If we open our hearts, begin to listen and file away the snapshots, then one day all of the black-and-white impressions in our minds will meld together to complete the clear, gloriously panoramic, intricately woven, and beautiful tapestry of the dog's nature and message.

This first stage, the beginning of awareness, marks the start of the journey, where small epiphanies of the dog's message are acknowledged, and in some measure understood; and represents the starting point and foundation upon which each dog begins to teach the message for spiritual growth. The dogs in your past, the dogs in your present, and the dogs in your future are contributors and instigators of this process. All patiently contribute to the deliverance of the messages of joy, truth, and love. Each dog rejoicing in your progression of understanding along the path of your journey.

Dogs speak to all mankind. The question is not to whom they speak, but who begins to listen. So as we begin to listen, we recognize the worth of the dog as a mentor by his true expressions of goodness; and as we compare them with our own, we find ours lacking. With this awareness and by his gentle nudging, we begin communication with his soul, and he with ours. Now the journey and the lessons begin. Listening brings us to the starting line where, without saying a word, the dog assumes his role as our guide and teacher along the way. As with any journey into unknown regions and unfamiliar terrain, the novice traveler must learn to trust the guide and, reciprocally, the guide and teacher must prove his worth. With each day, the dog proves that he is up to the task. As we become enlightened to the dog's inherent nature, as we begin the journey aware of the truth of their mission and their humble expression of their gifts, we cannot fail to realize and appreciate the attributes and attitudes of our truest friends.

The hope and the destiny intended for humanity is with our discovery and acceptance of the dog's messages and his expressions of the gifts: humility, forgiveness, tolerance, and loyalty. With our acceptance of these gifts, hope springs eternal and our destiny awaits us just ahead over the horizon. *And the journey begins.*

ATTITUDES AND ATTRIBUTES

If you can start the day without caffeine,
If you can get going without pep pills,
If you can always be cheerful, ignoring aches and pains,
If you can resist complaining and boring people with your troubles,
If you can eat the same food every day and be grateful for it,
If you can understand when your loved ones are too busy to give you any time,
If you can overlook it when your loved ones take it out on you when, no fault of yours, something goes wrong,
If you can take criticism and blame without resentment,
If you can ignore a friend's limited education and never correct him,
If you can resist treating a rich friend better than a poor friend,
If you can face the world without lies and deceit,
If you can conquer tension without medical help,
If you can relax without liquor, and sleep without the aid of drugs,
If you can say honestly that deep in your heart you have no prejudiced against creed, color, religion....,
Then, my friend, you are almost as good as your dog.

Anonymous

Man can find no fault in dogs, only in himself, and these he freely bestows upon them. Some humans try to reflect and force their foibles upon the dog, and unfortunately, sometimes, they succeed. But the origin of the bad-rap given to dogs is truly attributable to the very creature who announces it and attaches the label. The dog, however, comes to us naturally pure and godly, but what we impose upon his nature is sometimes suspect and often quite sinful and sinister. Yet he remains, deep down, a true saint, all things considered, with four attributes remaining constant no matter what influences we throw at him.

To the wonderfully enlightening and truthful, anonymous quote, I modestly add:

And if you can humbly and freely give yourself to humanity without seeking reward…
And if you can unfailingly forgive transgressions against you…
And if you can refuse to judge others; remain uplifting, always offering tenderness and understanding…
And if you can remain steadfast loyal to your cause and the meaning in your life…
Then, my friends, you may come to close to the 'Attitude and Attributes' of your dog.

Chapter 12

CHOICES OF ATTITUDE

Dr. Hal Urban wrote a great people book, *"Life's Greatest Lessons, 20 Things That Matter"*. A good read for young and old alike. One of the chapters deals with choices we humans are free to make; decisions, because of our free will, which can affect and shape a purposeful and productive life. In that chapter, Dr. Urban, holding a doctorate in education and psychology, demonstrates a lack of knowledge about animals, dogs in particular, when he states…

…*"you watch the family dog, an elephant in the zoo, or a mountain goat in the Andes, you'll see they do essentially the same thing. They eat, sleep, seek shelter and breed. Those are all instincts. That's what they live by. Their sole purpose is to survive… We have more than instincts. We have the ability to choose. That's what separates humans…And if we don't* (choose) *then we are no better off"*.

I have quoted Dr. Urban directly rather than paraphrasing his remarks because I couldn't begin to summarize such unfounded, inaccurate remarks about dogs. Urban's book illustrates a thorough understanding of human students in various stages struggling with the lessons of human development, and his book is loaded with good human advice concerning living in a purely human world. However, he doesn't seem to know a thing about dogs. Hopefully, his comment about dogs, the only statement in his book that is unfounded, indicates merely an innocent ignorance of a dog's essence. His book is an invaluable guide for humans, but to state that dogs have no faculties of choice, reacting only by instinct, a word usually suggesting only primitive intelligence, indicates a singularly narrow view of the dog's nature, even for a doctor of *human* psychology.

When scientists, psychologists, and philosophers discuss humans, they credit decisions made and actions taken to a conscious choice, while calling deliberate actions by animals merely instinct. Such a narrow, myopic view brings to mind the Seventeenth century philosopher Rene' Descartes and his principle of Dualism, which states that the *being* of a human contains two distinct parts: the mind and the body. The body, merely a machine, demonstrates motion and extension and adheres to the laws of physics. While the mind, having no motion or extension relevant to the laws of physics, acts as the center of thinking and feeling. According to Descartes, the mind interacts with and sends instructions through the mechanisms of the body via the pineal gland: a gland he erroneously believed only humans possessed. Further, he concluded the pineal gland was the seat of the soul and based on this theory alone assumed that the soul was non-existent in any creature non-human. Therefore, he believed no soulless creature could think, or feel pain. In order to prove his theory, declaring dogs nothing but machines without feelings, absent a pineal gland or a soul, he eviscerated a live dog shackled to a gurney. One can only imagine the dismal failure of that experiment!

And by the way, dogs do have a pineal gland. This is the same philosopher remembered for his so-called erudite proposition that claimed proof of his and our existence by his shallow and banal declaration, *"I think, therefore I am"*. Descartes wasn't just a near-sighted charlatan, but a cruel one at that! Yet, many humans actually revered Descartes' philosophical drivel expounded in his treatises.

I certainly don't mean to imply that Hal Urban's benign, misinformed remark places him in the same cruel, archaic company of Rene' Descartes, but many times humans erroneously give credence unduly to their own kind as long as their views or statements place man on a pedestal separating him from other creatures. By his remark, I think Dr. Urban uncharacteristically, unwittingly, and innocently placed himself in *this* category. And if he were to read this book, I think he might reconsider '*the family dog*'.

I like Urban's book. It's a good primer for humans who need to learn how to be truthful, productive, respectful, loving members of society. It's a good book for people thirteen to eighty who retain teenage tendencies and most of us need to read it, listen to his messages, and follow his advice. But dogs do not; for Dr. Urban merely would be '*preaching to the choir*'.

In each of the following four chapters I have taken the liberty to include Dr. Urban's statement about the family dog or have quoted from his book a constructive and cognitive choice: a choice, he states, which is available to humans, but not to dogs. You decide if the statement is accurate and if each choice remains exclusive.

Chapter 13

HUMILITY AND HUMANITY

"you watch the family dog, an elephant in the zoo, or a mountain goat in the Andes, you'll see they do essentially the same thing. They eat, sleep, seek shelter and breed."

Hal Urban

Pride - egotistical conceit - the first and most scornful of the Seven Deadly Sins, does not rear its ugly head in the character of the dog. You will not see a dog egotistically promoting himself at the expense and detriment of others. No matter how noble, no matter how handsome, you will not find a narcissistic dog looking in the mirror admiring himself, and you don't find the dog putting on 'airs' for us or to other dogs. Neither are dogs concerned a whit for our appearance of dress or face, or that of another dog, being solely preoccupied with the scent and essence of the other end. For they know that's the way to 'get at' the true core of one's character. And true character, as the dog knows, has nothing to do with the façade of appearance and pomp, but has much to do with a good sniff.

Dogs are unassuming creatures who like being who they are; and only in that sense do dogs possess pride in their character and goodness, but they lack self-absorbed conceit. However, this unassuming, trusting nature makes them somewhat susceptible to a *degree* of human manipulation; some good, but unfortunately some bad. The product of the bad manipulation never fails to be reported, disparaging the character of dogs, but rarely identifies the true villain. A vicious Pit Bull always makes the news, but seldom does his malevolent keeper and trainer. The dog is exterminated but the true cause, the human, often roams free to impose their cowardly, corrupt personality onto another dog or inflict their cruelty on a child, or another unassuming human incapable of defending himself.

Viciousness is not inborn in a dog, but humility and trustfulness are, and such are the hallmarks of the dog's nature. And if this nature is explored correctly, or at least not sabotaged or perverted by humans, it manifests itself in humanity.

How many police *monkeys* bravely penetrate a building where an armed criminal waits to shoot to kill anything that moves? When was the last time you saw a *sheep* leading a blind man across the street and through traffic? A 'service' *goat* doesn't aid infirmed, cripple humans with household needs and daily attentions. It wasn't a team of *elephants* that mushed through snow and ice, suffering raging winds, enduring forty-degree-below-zero temperatures, traveling one thousand miles from Anchorage to Nome, Alaska in five and one-half days delivering a vaccine to a village of people dying from diphtheria. And television broadcasts during and after September 11 were not reporting the brave and valiant effort of *cats* with torn and bloody paws trying to claw their way through concrete and steel debris to locate and save humans.

The noble dog comes to us with humility and this attribute and attitude is palpable and somewhat malleable, but remains indomitable. For in achieving the highest level of humility (the likes of which Jesus possessed) strength and power are attained through a connection with God; resulting in a diminution of the feeling of self importance, while simultaneously experiencing an awareness of - and relying on - a connection with a *far greater power within*. Becoming an instrument of God, humbly the dog demonstrates, *'Thy will be done'*. With the goodness and bravery of his humble, unassuming character and with eager enthusiasm unmatched by any creature on earth, he chooses to offer and sacrifice his existence for the benefit of humanity. I don't pretend to know what mental exercises the dog uses to arrive at the decision - the *choice* being not just his, but also God's. But, I do know that it falls on our shoulders to deserve it, as do all unselfish, sacrificial acts benefiting humanity: Now or two thousands years ago.

In the language of Aramaic, the original, forgotten language of the Bible, humble means 'lack of sinful pride, unassuming'. And from the Aramaic translation of the Bible, these words ring true about dogs:

"Blessed are the humble, for theirs is the Kingdom of Heaven"

Chapter 14
FORGIVENESS - THE SINS OF OTHERS

"We're free to choose how to handle adversity. We can allow ourselves to be crushed, to give up… Or we can choose to look for a source of strength within us… to make the most out of what life deals us."   Hal Urban

Unlike humans, dogs can't hold on to a grudge. They just can't seem to get their paws around the concept of bitterness like humans can. *Temporarily,* dogs can be crushed by constant cruelty or stunned and injured by hate. But they don't let the results of cruelty or hate take control, producing bitterness, destroying or dominating their attitude and attribute of forgiveness.

Years ago, while in my late teens, I liked hunting, persuaded at a young age to revere the activity as part of our collective heritage. I now reject the practice and haven't fired a weapon at an animal for over thirty-seven years. I suppose I could again if forced to by starvation, but, thankfully, that is not the case. In years past, to my shame and regret, I stood around and watched hunters unmercifully beat their dogs for disobeying or failure to perform up to standards. I watched as the poor dogs suffered and cowered under the cruelty and a few minutes later slink toward the human, attempting to lick the very hand that delivered the cruelty. The day I stopped hunting I watched an eager but nonconforming dog shot and left for dead in the field. I hear stories of hunters in the next county getting together at the end of the hunting season to practice target shooting. The targets are their non-productive dogs. They cull out the weak, the elderly, and the nonconforming, and lessen the food bill during the off-season. Before I go any further with this, I want to say that many hunters venerate their dogs and would never think of executing such a hideous act. However, some do. And so we get to the story and fate of Bobbie Sue, the three-legged Beagle.

Dave and Margie, avid and devoted dog lovers, live in the rural area of Urbana, Virginia, surrounded by hunters. A long time friend, Margie calls several times a week during hunting season sorrowfully irritable over sighting malnourished or dead hunting hounds along the rural roads. Margie, a lady made tough by the vicissitudes of life, has a heart of mush when ill-fated situations involve animals, especially dogs. Unbridled compassion opens their home to many feeble, homeless dogs allowing many of these dogs to find loving homes, and soon another would appear.

One day Margie answered the phone to hear the person on the other end explain the situation down at the animal shelter. A beagle had been brought in by a human who happened by and saw the dog hobbling along the side of the road struggling to drag herself into a thicket; presumably to die painfully from the gunshot wound that had badly mangled her right hind leg. She rushed to the shelter where she was told that the curator planned to euthanize the dog because of the injury. Margie knew what she had to do and didn't hesitate. After a brief phone call to her husband, she adopted the dog right away and then rushed to the Vet. The emergency operation performed saved the dog but not the leg. Several shot-pellet wounds made repair impossible, necessitating the amputation of the lower portion of Bobbie Sue's leg up to her knee. Over the span of two weeks, the dog convalesced but remained weak and fragile showing little emotion. Margie and Dave were concerned. They knew while the physical wound would heal, the wound to the dog's heart might not. They knew the life of the hunting dog: caged ninety-nine percent of the time in a pen with several dozen of their kind, without emotional contact with humans except during hunting season. And even then, any emotions likely heading their way might resemble the same sort Bobbie Sue experienced the day she was shot. Living a life of neglect and then being shot certainly doesn't contribute favorably to a well-balanced mental attitude, even for the resilient nature of a dog. How would Bobbie Sue interact with the other three dogs, and with Dave and Margie?

But not to worry. Bobbie Sue recovered physically and mentally. The hunting dog shot and left for dead by a cruel human, recovered and turned into a three-legged, pure bundle of joy and affection; joyfully playing and roughhousing with the other dogs in the family and showing a special fondness for Dave, the true apple of her eye and the object of her constant attention and love. Interestingly, she bonded tightly to Dave. Most keepers of hunting dogs are men and most hunters are also, but Bobbie Sue chose to shower Dave with her love. Even Margie reluctantly admitted the dog loved Dave much more than her. Maybe Bobbie Sue felt Dave's inherent guilt over another man's sin and cruelty, and heart-to-heart, soul-to-soul forgave him for the sins of one of his 'kind'. Perhaps she even rationalized the shooting; somehow convincing herself the shooter accidentally wounded her. Even so, how many humans would forgive an accident that caused the loss of their leg? Most would remain bitter and unforgiving.

We will never know what mental exercises Bobbie Sue went through before or after the day she was shot and left for dead. We can't speculate what *'source of strength within'* she relied on allowing her to forgive, but we do know she made *'the most out of what life'* handed her. And, we do know her playful, joyous antics proved she possessed the will to overcome and *'handle adversity'*, physical and mental. By her demonstration of love, we do know she forgave Dave and his 'kind'. Who among us walking on two legs can equal the forgiving nature of our companions walking on four, or in this case three? We have to go back in history two thousand years to find Him, *or* look beside us now, discovering our dog.

Basic instinct or a conscious choice? Definitely a choice: for dogs openly and honestly expose their character within, and by demonstration reveal their *choices* consciously made. They cannot do, or be, otherwise!

In the dictionary, we find the meaning of the word 'Forgiveness', n. cessation of resentment for or against; to give pardon, relief from debt.

My definition - forgiveness: a Heavenly virtue unfailingly practiced and personified by dogs; and by Another, two thousand years ago and now.

Chapter 15

THE CHOICE OF JUDGMENT

"We are free to choose how to treat other people. We can put them down, or we can lift them up. We can be self-centered... or we can be kind and helpful."   Hal Urban

The most sinisterly dark and damaging part of human nature around which conflict and turmoil gathers is our urgent and perpetual rush to judge others. Our quickness to disparage other creatures, humans included, dominates our daily regimen so completely that throwing off the habit is like breaking the urge to inhale. No tendency is more prevalent among us and none engenders more animosity between us. Our gun slinging, quick draw tendency to pull out our judgment and fire mental and sometimes physical invectives at another is caused solely by our self-centered confusion of reality.

Individually and collectively, something inside of us tells us that anyone who does not look like us, think like us, or live like us is wrong. We call this something ego; and ego, by its own nature and definition isolates us from all other things human, spiritual, and natural. Ego promotes and perpetuates the illusion of separateness and takes us down a road leading the opposite way from spirituality and oneness. For in reality, which ego obscures, we are all one, inextricably connected in union with God, nature and the universe. Inherently, our soul knows of this connection, but uncontrolled clouds of ego stunt the soul's spiritual growth and smother its acuity. In the physical field of our relative mind, ego plants the seed of isolation, fertilizes resentment, and judgment grows rampant.

Not only is ego the vehicle by which we determine ourselves separate and superior to another, but the pervasiveness of the practice compels low self esteem in others and, ironically, in its owner. Convinced we are superior or surrendering to inferiority, we move to withdraw within ourselves thereby creating ego boundaries, solitary confinement, and despair. All which preclude spiritual (and mental) growth.

The non-judgmental dog owns no ego, belonging to nature and remaining one with God. And so the dog appears; and if we listen, he will by example quiet our ego, leading us to a more tolerant disposition. Also, he soothes our inferiority caused by the effects of ego by ignoring our shortcomings while imploring demonstration of our goodness and worth. Even scientists, and other anti-anthropomorphics, seeing the evidence, admit that dogs adeptly apply an educational philosophy and psychological premise: The premise and practice of uplifting the esteem and confidence of another by disregarding limitations and shortcomings while extolling qualities and virtues.

With a non-judging attitude 'Zoom', a Welsh Corgi, and a certified reading therapy dog, and the many like him, expertly and patiently listens as children, reacting positively to his tolerant disposition, read to him without impediment as Zoom rests his head beside them on a pillow. Reading teachers see a marked improvement of reading skills when a remedial student reads to a non-judgmental Therapy Dog. Interestingly, dogs evade scientific explanation by proving themselves masterful practitioners of a purely human (or so humans consider) concoction: the scientific premise of *'the self fulfilling prophecy'*. Dogs may not fully comprehend the scientific term imbued with human particulars, but they use it very effectively as shown by their non-judgmental attitude, their kind and helpful participation in 'Reading Therapy', and the Prison Pet Partnership Program.

The Prison Pet Partnership Program began in 1981 in a Washington State women's prison has been the subject on NBC's "What's Right In America" and featured on Nature's "Extraordinary Dogs." Several years ago both programs documented a program ongoing in the Washington State women's prison system demonstrating a touching, symbiotic relationship between dogs and humans, and just another benefit of the primordial bond formed years ago. However, this time the interaction, for once, benefited the humans and *dogs* equally. The program adopts homeless dogs, rescuing them from local animal shelters, many of the dogs barely escaping impending extermination. The dogs go from one prison to another; but at their new home they find a chance to prove the goodness of their inherent nature and more. The dogs are assigned to inmates who train them to become companions, or Service and Seizure therapy dogs for disabled humans with Multiple Sclerosis, Autism and other handicaps. They learn to retrieve items (shoes, keys, etc.). They are taught to help brace a weak human attempting to stand from a sitting position. The dogs learn proper protocol for guarding their human during a seizure and helping them stand after the fall. The dogs even learn how to open doors for their humans, and a myriad of daily tasks able-bodied humans take for granted. Dogs not suited to become Service Companions are taught social graces and basic obedience skills and reintroduced back into society as 'Paroled Dogs', and the demand for them and the service dogs is overwhelming. Inmates are totally responsible for training the dog with supervision twice a week by a trainer who monitors progress and provides instruction to the inmates. The dog and the inmate remain inseparable as long as the training lasts, usually eight to twelve months. Constant companions, they eat together, sleep together, and learn together: the dog as the student, the inmate as the teacher. But something unexpected predictably happened: The student became a teacher.

As their dog graduated from the program leaving their instructor to begin their appointed duty, the inmates revealed the impact the dogs had on their attitude and life. Sobbingly wiping tears from their eyes, inmates told of the loving bond that developed between them. The inmates said they found in the dog a loving, trusting companion; but most importantly, they experienced a non-judgmental acceptance and uplifting tenderness for the first time in their life. Their dog, being a dog, refused to judge the human when others humans had. Without prejudice, the dogs looked past society's 'scarlet letter', ignored the inmate's past shortcomings, and pleaded for their kindness and love, and both were given. And in return, as they always do, the dogs reciprocated with love and tenderness, refusing to judge a life that at one time had gone astray. Disregarding shortcomings while discovering virtues, the dogs began laying the foundation for building and regaining self-esteem.

In addition, another phenomenon was manifested. The inmates probably for the first time in their life found a purpose. They were given a chance to perform a noble humanitarian endeavor by training their dog to help a fellow human in need. And probably for the first time, their self-esteem, given a much needed boost, flourished and grew, and personal redemption was imminent. As a result, another benefit became evident. Recidivism among the participating inmates is non-existent. After release from prison, no participating inmate has committed another crime.

The director of the Pet Partnership program in Washington State claims over eight-hundred dogs have graduated from the program since its inception in 1981, going on to perform their humanitarian function. The prototype program has been so successful that twenty states now have similar programs in both men's and women's prisons. The dogs once again find a human need, and, once again, they fill it admirably. Not only for the disabled, but also for the inmates they refused judge, improving their battered self-esteem, uplifting and transforming their lives with compassion and love.

All of this made possible by a non-judgmental creature, containing an unprejudiced heart, devoid of ego.

The Choice of a True Friend

Going back to Urban's quote, we find the words 'self-centered', another word for ego. He uses the words in an 'either or' context, suggesting, *"We can be self-centered or we can be kind and helpful,"* but we can't be both, and he is right. By definition, we cannot be humanitarian if we remain isolated from others by ego, which by its strictest definition means **'I'**. When all that matters is the **'I'**, then nothing else does; not helping another, not being kind to another, not lifting up another, and in essence, not humanity. The **'I'** is separate and isolated. The **'I'** looks down from a self-constructed platform built of a framework of papier-mâché that can hardly support the heavy weight of *one* laden with ego, leaving no measure of area or support for another. Ego, and the resultant isolation it causes, to some degree or another, precludes a true friendship. A true friend doesn't rush to judgment, never puts their friends *'down'*, and always stands ready to lend a helping hand. And, above all, is tolerant and *'kind'*, being so without the self-centered requirement of all this being returned.

With our perception clouded by ego and the fog of isolation it causes, would we truly recognize a good friend if he appeared before us? Would we reciprocate in kind? And could ego allow a true friendship to endure once we encounter it? Unfortunately, some of us move through life without having an extraordinarily good friend. How many of our friendships endure the test of time and quality? And worse: how many of us qualify as a true friend, passing the test ourselves? Because of ego, true friendship is a two-way street humans find difficult to negotiate. Always 'treating others the way we would like to be treated' can prove nearly impossible. It has been said that if we live our entire life counting among our gifts but one true friend, then we are truly blessed. Being or keeping a true friend is difficult because we don't choose to step down from our platform of ego long enough to be in touch with the qualities comprising a good friend, *and* because we egotistically refuse to take the time to consider what qualities are required within us to become one.

Consider one who always *chooses* to treat you with dignity and respect, never demonstrating an unkind feeling toward you regardless of your failure to reciprocate. Constantly, your friend expresses a positive attitude toward you, always revealing optimism, always greeting your appearance with true joy, and truly rejoicing in your presence. And when you are feeling down and depressed over what life throws at you, whether a minor setback or a life-changing disaster, your true friend is always there to urge you to find joy and pleasure in life if you are ready to accept it, and quietly shows empathy when you aren't. Someone who can read your emotions in time of distress and appropriately cheers you up; or, if all you wish is quiet compassion and companionship, will curl up with you and quietly share your tears, and tip-toe next to your heart and remain there with steady comfort and acquiescent sympathy. When you suffer from insecurity, having suffered under the weight of another man's ridicule or society's criticism and judgment, or simply when you question your value and doubt your self-esteem, your unselfish friend never fails you. Choosing to ignore your self-constructed shortcomings and your broken self-esteem shattered by others, your true friend never fails to lift you up with tenderness and love, demonstrating a true belief in your worthiness. Loving you for who and what you are, nudging you to realize your intrinsic value, providing inspiration, and uplifting your self-esteem.

What would you choose to call such a gift - a true endowment who resolutely decides to accompany you in life, steadfastly walking with you through thick and thin, supporting you in good times and bad, always willing to answer your call and your need for comfort, tenderness, and kindness - your truest, best friend? An indispensable companion? You are '*free to choose*' to call *it* whatever name you desire. Your dog will answer to that call, too!

In the physical world, no two creatures *choose* to cross the humanly constructed species barrier to the same degree as the dog and *some* men. But the dog jumps the fence with more agility, carrying none of the weight of the physical world's heaviest baggage: ego.

Chapter 16

THE CHOICE OF LOYALTY

"We are free to choose our own purpose. We can wander aimlessly or we can search for a meaning in life, and then live according to it. We can live to please ourselves, or we can find a cause that's greater..."
Hal Urban

Dogs want to be with us. They thrive on the union and so do we. We know the relationship began many thousands of years ago and scientists have evidence substantiating the bond. The benefits each party receives are evident in many ways, but the weight of the scales tip drastically in favor of the humans; unquestionably, dogs benefit man's life more than any other creature on earth and, unfortunately, more than we do theirs. And through the years, the dog remains the linchpin of the union despite man's frequent failure to reciprocate. This bond, often unilateral, strictly sustained by dogs demonstrates the next attitude and attribute - loyalty.

When we are lost, separated from them physically or spiritually, dogs *choose* to find us; because, we mean so much to them and because they know we need them, even if we don't realize it.

Joker *

In 1958, the Associated Press published a well-documented story of a Cocker Spaniel's journey to unite with his human. During World War II, his human received

orders to report for duty in the South Pacific. Faced
with no alterative he left Joker behind with his family in
Pittsburg, California. According to the A.P. report, the
dog after two weeks of refusing to eat, and despondent
over the separation, *chose* to disappear. Several days later,
Joker showed up thirty miles away from home in Oakland,
where two Army doctors documented their attempt to
capture him. Joker managed to escape and found stowaway
passage on an Army transport ship headed for the South
Pacific. When discovered on board he was befriended
by a dog loving army officer who kept him as the boat's
mascot. Joker's ship traveled to several ports along the way
to their destination and at every stop Joker appeared on
deck judiciously sniffing the air and astutely surveying his
surroundings, but he made no attempt to jump ship. When
the ship reached another destination in the South Pacific,
Joker immediately, without hesitation, abandoned ship,
ran ashore, and soon was barking joyously at the feet of an
astounded Army Captain Stanley C. Raye, the human who
left his dog in Pittsburg, California. *Joker's lost human finds
him again.*

Lord *

On a beach, Paquita Soler of Gandia, Spain befriended a weak and starving, small stray dog by sharing a
sandwich with him. However, at sixty-seven years old, she
was somewhat reluctant to add to her life the responsibility
of caring for a young and starving abandoned dog. As she

tried to walk away, the small, bedraggled dog followed imploring to her kindness. Finally she caved in, and deciding to give him a chance at life, picked up the dog and together they returned home. With the results of several Vet visits, and provided with a loving home, the dog she named 'Lord' regained his health and became an integral part of her life and a constant companion. Paquita soon learned she had a serious illness requiring at least two months of treatment in Paris to affect the cure. Faced with a serious health problem but anxious over the welfare of Lord she decided to leave him with friends in Montpellier, France.

With the successful medical treatments concluded sooner than expected, she returned in January 1993 to her friend's house in France to retrieve her beloved dog. Instead of a joyous reunion, she was told the grieving dog slipped away one night several weeks after she had left him, never to be seen again. Heartbroken, Paquita returned home to Spain about five hundred miles away, with horrific thoughts of Lord's fate going through her mind.

In June 1993, she heard a noise at her window and upon investigating found Lord standing there starving and bedraggled, reminiscent of the same condition as when he first found her on the beach a year before. But this time his paws and pads were bleeding from the five hundred mile, six-month journey down Spain's Mediterranean coast. A demanding trek which required traversing mountains, traveling through dense forests, and along busy, dangerous roads. *But, Lord's wayward companion has returned to his love.*

Nick *

In 1979, the local newspaper ran the astounding story of Nick a female German Shepherd who traveled from southern Arizona to Selah, Washington after being separated from her human, Doug Simpson, while on a camping trip. After searching the inhospitable terrain of the southwestern desert for two weeks, the reluctant Simpson returned home to Washington State without his dog. We can only imagine Simpson's disbelief when Nick showed up in terrible shape at his front door four months later, starving, and emaciated. Her pitiful condition was quite understandable since she had traveled two thousand miles through some of the most hostile terrain in the country on her journey to reunite. *Doug Simpson reunites with Nick's love.*

Bobbie *

One of the most famous as well as the most documented journey is the amazing story by Bobbie, the incredible Collie who in 1923 traveled two thousand documented miles to reunite with his owners, Mr. and Mrs. Frank Brazier of Silverton, Oregon. While the Braziers and Bobbie were in Westcott, Indiana visiting friends, a twist of fate separated the dog from his family. After extensive searching, the Braziers placed ads in the local newspapers offering rewards. They drove the countryside asking numerous people if by chance they had encountered Bobbie. The Braziers hopelessly ended their search and reluctantly returned home to Oregon. Seven months later the big Collie appeared at the front door of the Brazier's home and bolting past Mrs. Brazier, ran upstairs, and jumped into the bed with the sleeping Frank, licking his face and howling for joy. *Bobbie's long, lost love finds him, again.*

The astounding journey home caused the president of the Oregon Humane Society to launch an investigation to explain, verify, and track the route of the odyssey. Hundreds of letters poured in substantiating sightings of Bobbie in various parts of the country heading west on his amazing journey home. Accounts poured in from many strangers who befriended the starving and freezing dog. Letters described the bloody pads of Bobbie's paws so wounded and raw that bones were exposed. Other accounts related incidents of Bobbie being hit by a tractor and others described the day he was kicked by a horse. Bobbies' physical condition and examination verified all accounts. So extensive were the eyewitness accounts and the letters from people who encountered or befriended Bobbie during his trip, that Charles Alexander documented the incredible journey in his book: *"Bobbie, a Great Collie from Oregon"*

In the late summer of 2004, I, along with my dog family, started on a journey across country. Our journey began about as far east as you can get without getting wet: Nags Head, North Carolina, and ended about as far west as you can go without swimming: Monterey, California. On our way west we took the northern route. We traveled through the rolling blue grass of Kentucky, across the wide expanse of the Mississippi and the Missouri rivers, through Indiana. On to the Great Plains, through the Black Hills, and Bad Lands of South Dakota, as we crossed the 'Big Mo' again. We continued through the desolate mountainous regions of Wyoming, where the only thing you saw for fifty miles was an occasional antelope, and oil wells. We crossed the Rockies of Utah and Nevada, passing the Great Salt Lake and desolate salt flats, past Lake Tahoe and through the great fertile valleys of California on the way to the Pacific Ocean. On the way back, we traveled the southern route traversing the great Mojave Desert, rolling past the Grand Canyon of Arizona and through the rocky terrain of time sculptured rock formations and tabletop mesas of New Mexico. Through the barren flatlands of Texas on through the swamps and bayous of the Gulf States, past the Gulf of Mexico and back up the Eastern Seaboard.

On the way westward and back again, I kept thinking to myself and sometimes remarking out-loud to the dogs about the arduous task the pioneers undertook when attempting to transverse this great country in covered wagons powered by a team of mules. Traveling across wide, raging rivers, treacherous mountain passes, dangerous and desolate plains, and hot, expansive and forbiddingly dry deserts. You have to hand it to our pioneer ancestors who undertook this journey seeking the promise of a better, more meaningful life. Many were led by guides or traveled with wagon trains escorted by experienced wagon-masters. But we can only imagine what life on the trail threw at them. As I and my dogs traveled daily westward in the comfort of an RV through awesomely beautiful but hostile terrain, I marveled at the fortitude and determination of travelers heading the same direction, through the same terrain, one hundred and fifty years earlier.

The westward track of the early pioneers and the hardships they endured was not hard to imagine even as I rolled along interstate highways doing sixty-five miles an hour in the comfort of the RV. Now try to imagine Bobbie, the great Collie from Oregon, following the same terrain as the pioneers and the same route I was traveling; but without a road map or an experienced guide, as he traveled two thousand miles across raging rivers, desolate badlands, and snow-covered treacherous mountain trails. Upon the daily end of our journey, I and my dogs stopped at campgrounds, hooked up to utilities providing comfort, cooked our dinner, enjoyed the scenery and slept in a comfortable bed (all five of us), and awoke safe and rested in the shelter of the RV. What daily and nightly dangers and hourly sacrifices and discomforts did Bobbie face on his way from Indiana to Oregon in order to unite with the human he loved, the human who went missing seven months earlier? Or try putting yourself on the four paws of Nick, the female German Shepherd, and feel the cutting cruel rocks and jagged stones of the hot and foreboding floor of the southwestern desert on your journey of two thousand miles from Arizona to Washington State to find your human lost in the desert four months earlier.

Some skeptics of Bobbie's (and the other dog's) ability to choose his purpose may point to the dog's basic instinct which instigated the journey and insured his survival. But I contend that along with instinct and strength to survive, he possessed an attribute that predicated a *choice*: loyalty. From the time he figured he was separated from his human, Bobbie made a conscious decision, a choice. Not a choice to survive, for his instinct and his strength and perhaps his cunning insured that, but rather a choice consciously made to reunite with the object of his love. For no amount of instinct, strength, or even luck could singly compel, perpetuate, and accomplish the journey Bobbie undertook. No, what led Bobbie (and the others) to find his human, guided and motivated him through the perils of his journey was not a will to survive, but a *choice* to reunite. The manifestation of will motivated a choice. With each painful, bloody step he took along his two thousand mile journey, every time his torn and bloody feet painfully hit the ground, every peril he encountered and overcame, every obstacle he came across and surmounted was done by choice. He *chose* to reunite with his beloved human; a choice compelled by an attribute and attitude of loyalty, and a whole bunch of love.

Accounts of dogs reuniting after traveling incredible physical distances present only part of the story. Many times a dog's sense of devotion continues after his human journeys to another realm. Monuments immortalizing such famous accounts stand in commemoration of 'Tip', the famous sheep dog found in emaciated condition in the snow covered highlands of Derbyshire, U.K., at the side of her dead human, eighty-one year old Joseph Tagg, fifteen weeks after they both went missing in the moors on December 12, 1953. And a monument stands near a churchyard in Edinburgh, Scotland containing a statute of

Greyfriars Bobby, a terrier who slept on his human's grave every night for fourteen years until *his* death in 1872.

And now for the rest of the story: the saddest part. Many dogs stand ready to take on another type of journey, one equally incredible: the journey to reach across the minute *or* the infinite distance between two hearts. But, unfortunately, many times the journey is over before it can start. Last year's neglected Christmas gift that remains chained outside sleeping in a lonely wooden box night after night strains at his chain to begin his journey. The misunderstood dog deposited at the pound by humans unwilling to devote the time to understand imploringly stares through steel bars begging to start his journey. Numerous dogs stand ready to start the odyssey, but find themselves in situations that deny the opportunity to begin it. What a shame to waste their incredible gift of devotion and loyalty by denying them their *choice* to give it.

We humans have a ways to go in our process of connecting with our compassion for all creatures great and small. However, it is a good sign that we celebrate Bobbie, Nick and the rest of the dogs mentioned and extol the noble dogs who take on journeys to remain with their humans by erecting monuments to the loyalty of Greyfriars Bobby and Tip. But I suspect that dogs wonder what all the fuss is about, their loyalty and devotion being so natural and their desire to be with us so intense. Imploringly, they ask us to realize that the dog quietly lying at our feet or the uncelebrated one we have chained or penned in the back-yard stand ready to undertake the same journey to reach or remain, regardless of the physical distance of one mile or thousands, or the minute or the immense space separating your hearts. They all have one commonality. They all choose to "*search for* their *meaning in life*" and they choose to travel a path to "*find a cause that's greater*". They all make a choice. They know we need them, and they choose to be loyal to that which means so much to them: us. All of us would be blessed if we could experience such dedication and loyalty. And all of us who walk with dogs are!

Just a note so you won't think I confused the facts about the dog's journeys recounted above or that the printer confused the ending line of each story. You may think the syntax *mistakenly* represents that the human finds the dog rather than the other way around. Right? Wrong! The syntax is not botched. The dogs were never lost; the humans were. The dog knew where *he* was, but the *human* just didn't know where the dog was. The dog found his human no matter what it took to do so. Kind of sounds like our wayward attitude toward God. He knows where *we* are, *we* just can't seem to locate Him. But devotedly, He will seek us out no matter what it takes, and *we* will find Him again. ***Kind of like a dog?***

Dr. Urban, please reconsider "*the family dog*".

AND GOD SAID...

"The Highest Thought is always that thought which contains joy. The Clearest Words are those words which contain Truth. The Grandest Feeling is that feeling which you call love".

"Mine is always your Highest Thought, your Clearest Word, your Grandest Feeling. Anything less is from another source". *
Therefore...

JOY, TRUTH, and LOVE are the subjects of the next three chapters and God's three salient messages delivered by the dog who represents by thoughts, expression, and deeds the personification of the terms. All we need to do is listen in order to participate in the experience the dog presents. Because...

"My most powerful messenger is experience and even this you ignore".

"And so I will continue sending you the same messages over and over again, throughout the millennia and to whatever corner of the universe you occupy. Endlessly will I send you My messages until you have received them and hold them close, calling them your own" *

I hope the following chapters will lead to a receptive response and guide you to experience the messages of Joy, Truth, and Love offered by dogs and hold their messages **and** the messenger 'close', truly 'calling them your own'.

* *"Conversations With God"*

111

Chapter 17

JOY

"Man is troubled by what might be called the Dog Wish, a strange and involved compulsion to be as happy and as carefree as a dog."   James Thurber

Joy - Stifled and Regained

We humans often confuse true joy with self-gratification, or the superficial satisfaction of ego, calling it joy. Such is not true joy, but only solitary indulgence. Contrastingly, a dog's nature contains and demonstrates the highest form of intrinsic joy. In addition, their temperament compels the simple, uninhibited expression of delight freely given without fear of rejection. Unlike our human pursuit of self-gratification through solitary indulgence, the pinnacle of joy can only be reached by the gratuitous expression of joy to, and with, others; and this is what dogs do so well. Without even a mere thought of self gratification, dogs show intrinsic joy without the necessity of applause, requiring only a slight nod of acknowledgement; and given this nod, they repay us with consistent effusions of true joy. Unfortunately, human cruelty can temporarily constrain and stifle a dog's joyfulness, but can never eliminate it permanently.   Observations of joy exhibited by racing Greyhounds shortly after their liberation and introduction to a loving family, and the joyful attitude demonstrated in a short time by my two terribly abused rescued dogs testify to a dog's steadfast desire to show-off their joy in spite of previous efforts by others to quell it. Even though our joy lacks the constancy and, most of the time, the purity and sublimity of the dog's joy, the human spirit, by creation, contains immense joy that begs to be unleashed and expressed but remains shackled by the constraints of the physical world and the opinion of its society. However, with the dog's help and by their example, we learn that our spirit's joy also cannot be permanently quelled or eradicated.

At a young age, we humans begin repressing our inborn joy. Watch young children raised in a loving family at play and notice their joyful antics and their innate willingness to express and receive joy without hesitation. Regrettably, it is the process of development society calls 'growing up' that stifles the spontaneous and innocent effusions of joy. Society sets conditions for our expressions of joy determining a time and a place for it and advising of consequences if protocol is not observed. Fearing society's censure, we learn to repress emotions and if we are not careful and well grounded, we abandon our inherent tendency to give and receive joy, an inevitable consequence of our journey through the physical world and unavoidable if we remain stuck there. All too often we accept the false reality of this condition without being aware that there is escape from this world and our dog is our road map and guide. Who among us, witnessing the true joy demonstrated by dogs, does not yearn to return to a time in our life when we also openly celebrated our own joy and gratuitously expressed it to others? If we pay attention to the dog's example and follow his lead, we will yearn to evolve and move toward his natural world. Briefly at first, as we leave the false realty of our physical world we are treated to a glimpse of the joy in his domain. So we begin a journey with our dog joyfully in the lead. And by undertaking the journey, we then discover along the way joy, given and received, and ultimately, at the journey's end, we find the result: our spirits again unite as one, and we have returned home. And the dog's contagious joy accomplishes the mission!

Joy - Given and Received

As I prepared to write this part of this chapter, I approached it pretty much the same way I had done previously. I scribbled my ideas and notes on several pieces of notebook paper which were then scattered around the house in various places or in my cluttered mind, some easy to retrieve some not. I would often forget were I had stashed these notes so I could find them (somewhat of a paradox). I know it sounds unorganized but this ritual seemed to work in the past so I stuck with it. But with this chapter, I seemed to face a difficult challenge: how was I going to describe the topic of joy without relying upon my personal experiences with dogs. If you remember in Chapter 2, I vowed this book would not contain anecdotal episodes from my forty-four year relationship with dogs. However, a problem arose. How could I concentrate on and explain the cheerful nature of dogs and the true joy they present without relating anecdotal episodes gathered from interaction? After careful consideration and much thought, I concluded this to be impossible. So, in this chapter I will have to stray from my intent to exclude personal experiences, for without them this chapter would be very difficult to write and be extremely esoteric in style and content. While I must stray from my original intent, I promise to keep this deviation to a minimum for the remainder of the book.

Finding a Home, Feeling at Home

After considering many stories of joy dogs have presented, I settled on a 'scattered note' which came to mind from years past, the spring of 1980 to be exact, and concerned two dogs who were not part of my family or, for that matter, any human family. They were strays. Neither born in, nor lived around, a human environment. True feral dogs.

I was working for a large marine construction company based in Columbus Georgia. One of their satellite offices was a vast construction yard consisting of about thirty acres located off the southern branch of the Elizabeth River in Chesapeake, Virginia. Several office trailers had been set up for various employees, managerial staff, and support personnel for the field operations in that area. The trailers were situated in a compound surrounded by many acres containing construction equipment, debris from bridges, piers, and other structures that, in times past, served their purposes but had become useless by design and function except for as a den for two black puppies and their mother.

Under a massive pile of demolished concrete bridge girders and deck slabs is where Rueben, the yard mechanic, first got a glimpse of the small canine family. Back in those days, especially with the vast acreage and remoteness of the construction yard, nobody thought about calling animal control, which would have meant death by the gas chamber for the puppies and their mom. The pups were about three months old when the mother disappeared never to be seen again. Concerned for their sustenance which I suspected may have consisted of, at best, an occasional wharf rat, I began delivering food to the den located about five hundred yards from the trailer compound. Every Monday through Friday, before leaving work I would stroll to the den hoping in vain to get a glimpse of the two puppies who were seldom seen only at a distance as they wandered around the vast area. But, the food I left on an old piece of rusted corrugated tin disappeared by the next day. After about two weeks of this ritual, I arrived one Monday morning at my office trailer to find both of the puppies sitting side-by-side on their haunches on the sparsely graveled parking space, noses pointing directly at the front of my car. I stopped the car short and began slowly getting out and with that both simultaneously turned in the same direction and trotted away slowly, heads turned slightly toward me as they disappeared around the trailer and among the myriad piles of debris, equipment, and overgrown weeds.

For about a month, I continued feeding every day at about the same time, depositing food on the same piece of tin along with fresh water in a Tupperware bowl brought from home. About two months after my first and only encounter with the two pups, I was called out of town to work on and deliver a bid on a large project in Wilmington, North Carolina. I would be away for about a week but I had left enough food with a yard employee so he could continue the daily meal. When I returned the following Monday week, to my surprise both the pups sat in the same spot on the gravel parking pad. To my amazement, this time they did not move as I exited the car. They remained on their haunches, noses pointing straight ahead, and one of them, I swear, was smiling. At first I was taken aback a little for I mistook, even for just a second, the toothy grin to be an act of aggression or perhaps a sign of rabies. But no aggression was shown by either and they calmly remained. Here sat two handsome pure black dogs weighing about twenty-five pounds, one with long shiny black fur, and the other with short hair, both boys. And the broad grin was emanating from the shorthaired fellow. Smiley, as I had aptly named him had the unique ability to lift and curl his upper lip showing his teeth in a smiling gesture as he greeted you. I had heard and read reports of dogs joyously greeting humans in this manner but I had never actually seen it. As I approached the two, talking gently while slowly walking the distance of about fifteen feet, the only movement they made was to stand, tales frantically wagging. As I got closer, Smiley contorted his torso, turning his head and rump to his left making sort of a half moon out of his body, while giving me a big smile. I approached closer and to my surprise, they let me slowly put my hand on their heads. They showed no fear, no anxiety, or reticence at all. Gingerly touching their head progressed to gently rubbing and, kneeling down in front of them, I started rubbing along the ears, working my way along their backs, and all the while Smiley grinning and wagging his tail to the same rhythm as Lucky, who began scratching the ground with his right hind leg. This was, I am sure, their first touch by a human. I could not have felt more honor and joy as I did at this moment, and one was actually smiling at me. Were these two feral dogs, Lucky and Smiley, glad to see me? Were they allowing me to caress them because of a pure sense of joy at my arrival? What a beautiful and joyous event. I had observed humpback whales, been scuba diving with blue-tip sharks, swam with dolphins, and I had been face to face (way too close) with a large barracuda. But few events in my life brought forth so much emotion and joy as this brief, initial encounter with Smiley and Lucky - and one was still grinning at me. I wondered if the same joy overwhelming me was at the same time overpowering these two dogs who had never felt the touch of a human, never heard a soft-spoken human utterance, and never felt human fingers gently parting their fur.

A more blissful moment I could not remember, nor, sadly at the time, did I truly understand its significance. And the encounters didn't stop here, in fact, from that day on, every morning I arrived at work, I was joyously greeted by their wagging tails, wriggling bodies, and Smiley's grin. My return from lunch was met with the same greeting, rain or shine, and both received belly rubs and joyous salutations.

Within a few days, Smiley and Lucky had become mascots of the compound. I moved the food and water to my office trailer and both took up residence under it.

Over the next three months, they grew and flourished to handsome dogs weighing about thirty pounds. As always in life, things change. I had been offered employment with another company and would resign. I regretted leaving the two dogs and seriously considered adopting them, but I lived in an apartment and my job required extensive travel. Still to this day, I am ashamed of myself for being so self-centered. As I said, I failed to understand the blissful initial encounter with Smiley and Lucky and the daily joy conveyed by their greetings and presence. It wasn't until I resurrected and recollected this scene for this book that I came to recognize the import of that event twenty-seven years ago. For as I re-created and re-enacted this event in my mind in order to put it down on paper, the true panoramic picture became evident. The obscure snapshots of Lucky and Smiley - the joyously grinning feral dog - melded together and rendered the panoramic tapestry. The bits and pieces of the mosaic came together.

An age-old phenomenon, begun thousands of years ago, was inscrutably and inexorably revived and continued. These two feral dogs, whose previous encounters with humans were indulged only from a distance maintained by fear and uncertainty, found themselves intrinsically joined in a bond formed in ancient times. In 1980, these two feral dogs were compelled to companionship by a simple need and a complex desire to be tenderly and joyfully touched by a human. And, they were obliged to give in return the true joy of friendship, a wagging tail, and a smile. What higher, more sincere form of joy could be offered or received?

Joy - Closer to now and closer to a fence

It is never too soon to begin a regimen of house protocol with any dog, especially with Bichons, for they have been known to be considerably difficult to train. Not because they are idiots but because they are highly intelligent and a little too much like humans. I think they realize that humans don't go outside to relieve themselves so why should they. To a Bichon the house belongs as much to them as to any human, and they treat it as their domain, which is fine except for the bathroom thing. When two-month old Sallie Mo, who is now nine years old, came home from New York and introduced to her new surroundings, she immediately was indoctrinated to the basics of home training. But the fourteen, eight inch high steps leading to the entrance of our house were too much for her short, little legs to handle. I feared that even if she valiantly attempted to negotiate them, which she did, she would 'end up ass over tea-cup' and hurt herself. She was just a little baby then, weighing in at only three pounds, and in personality, she remains unchanged today. As with all babies, her nature calls were frequent and untimely. So to reduce the number of my trips carrying her up and down the stairs, newspapers were placed on the wood floors of the dining room next to the far wall. She readily accepted the regimen and faithfully used the paper to dispense with her business. As she finished, she would receive joyous accolades, especially over a poop, from the humans of the house who, with hands clapping rapidly, would loudly and rapidly shout over and over again "good-good-good-good-good Girl! Hearing the exclamations she would bolt out of the dining room, wriggling her body and tail, twirling in circles reacting to the sound of the praises, and barking rapidly keeping time to the clapping and the words good-good-good-good-good...Girl! As she grew to handle the steps the unnecessary newspapers were removed, but to this day, she still selects a place to poop right up against the yard fence that must remind her of the wall in the dining room. With her task completed, she immediately bolts into a mad dash and runs under the veranda and through the sliding door to the breakfast room. And no matter what part of the house I might be in, she runs to me barking, wriggling and twirling in circles letting me know she has done a poop and to receive clapping and rapid and joyous exclamations of 'good-good-good-good-good Girl'! To this day, I never have a problem with her toiletry habits. And the joy instilled over a poop continues, *given and received*.

This seemingly incidental and unimportant story recounted here serves to illustrate a point. Sometimes in this thing we call life, joy is conceived, instilled, perpetuated, and returned by obscure, insignificant acts of one creature toward another. Think about this for a moment. If tiny, unimportant acts like the one described above can cause joy to be given and received, then try to imagine the contagious joy and happiness we all could create by the simple act of letting down our collective defenses, and deliberately living with the purpose of expressing joy for and to each other. Even over something as insignificant as a poop. For the beauty of joy is truly in its thought, expression, and reception; and its highest truth and grandest feeling (love) is its result.

Coming Home

When I leave home, and as I the lock the full-view storm door, my four dogs unfailingly take up their positions sitting on the other side, their heads following the movement of the vehicle as they watch me leave. Whether I arrive home after a brief jaunt up the road or a four-hour absence, I find my four dogs sitting at the door in the same position as when I left, waiting relentlessly for my return. And it doesn't matter if other humans remain at home to keep them company, they remain vigilant, all four staring thru the glass waiting. They will not abandon that door. So reluctant are they to abandon their post that during the summer I have to close the solid door when I leave to keep the heat generated from the scorching, afternoon rays of the sun from causing heat exhaustion. Each time I return all kinds of havoc breaks out as they see the vehicle pull into the driveway. Callie Lu and Puppy (a rescue from a hideous junkyard and cruel humans) are standing on their hind legs flailing at the glass door with their flying front paws, seemingly trying to paw through the glass. Sallie

Mo rapidly twirls around to her left in tight circles with a diameter no larger than the length of her short body. She twirls so rapid that she makes five complete turns within three seconds and she will continue making the circles until I enter. I have counted as many as seventeen revolutions. During this melee, Little It, a fifteen-year-old rescue Toy Poodle barks frantically and with so much gusto that his front paws leave the ground with each bark. As I enter Sallie stops twirling and begins barking along with Callie, who not so much barks but chirps in with a high pitched, fast, continuous yelping. And as I reach down to pet everybody, Little It grabs my hand in his mouth holding it gently as if to say 'you are not to leave again'. By this time, Puppy is running like a wild man through the house, into the kitchen through the dining room, around the table, and into the living room at break-neck speed. And, abruptly putting on brakes in the breakfast room, he jumps straight into the air like a rabbit and, landing on all fours, crouches down on his front paws, rump raised and tail wagging. After everyone settles down, which takes several minutes to play out, all are treated to a belly rub and joyous salutations. Such is always the greeting.

In years past, with beloved dogs now gone, the same vigil was kept at the door, and the greetings were essentially the same. Jock and Portia would sit on their rumps, like a squirrel does eating a nut, with their front paws held together rapidly clawing at the air, while Brutus galloped bouncingly around the house up and down on every piece of furniture barking all the while. He would end this frantic display by good-naturedly body slamming his mom, Mercedes, whose bark, containing so much enthusiasm, caused her front paws to lift off the floor with each gesture of happy greetings. And everyone received belly rubs and joyous salutations.

How many marriages or relationships would remain intact if partners were treated to such a joyous display upon returning home at the end of the day?

Going Home

"You think dogs will not be in heaven? I tell you, they will be there long before any of us."
Robert Louis Stevenson

In the past I have tried to discover what may transpire when 'our home coming' occurs as we move from this life to the next. Many 'new-age' books describing the other side have been perused, many books on 'near-death experiences' have been read, and the Bible has been consulted. All seem to describe essentially the same joyous and loving welcome we will receive when we again return to our true home. I don't think it farfetched or out of the question if, at our reunion, we are greeted by the Almighty who wearing Smiley's grin, twirls around in tight circles, runs frantically around the place and after everyone settles down, gently holds our hand and says, "you are not to leave again." Perhaps you think God too regal to display His pleasure in this manner, but I truly hope He doesn't think the same way. But if, by chance, He declines to jump high in the air like a rabbit at our appearance, this I know for sure. He will be flanked by Brutus, Mercedes, Portia, Jock, Smokey, Lucky, Smiley and all the rest who will be ready to begin the joyous, rambunctious greetings, providing the fun, and waiting for a belly rub and joyous salutations. Such will be the JOY of heaven and a heavenly homecoming.

JOY, n. 1. a feeling of great delight or happiness; elation. 2. a cause of keen pleasure or delight.

In the chapter on 'Listening', I urged you to put the character of man and his dogmas to the TEST. Do their teachings, words, thoughts, and deeds follow the example of 'The Master' and contain the highest and most sincere form of love, truth, and JOY?

Now consider your dog. Pay attention to the joy of his greetings and learn that his joy is contagious. Catch it and pass it on to another creature, even a human. Observe a puppy playing with a young child. View the wag of a dog's tail and discover the smiles of joy and elation radiating from his character and the grin of great delight emanating from yours.

Joy - given and received? I think the dog's essence pretty much sums it up.

Chapter 18

TRUTH

"The Almighty, who gave the dog to be the companion of our pleasure and toils, hath invested him with a noble nature, incapable of deceit"   Sir Walter Scott

'You will find the truth at the bottom of a bottomless pit'. That's a line spoken in a movie I saw many years ago. I forget the title and the name of the actor who delivered the statement, but the comment remained intact in my mind, for no statement so accurately and succinctly defines the grueling task of finding truth in our society.

Truth is seldom found in man's world because truth is seldom found in man. I challenge you to find the needle of truth in a haystack of verbiage created by pandering politicians: men and women who belie their true convictions, if they possess any at all. Who willingly adopt any persona, eagerly assume any character, and readily change their beliefs to reflect the weather vane of shortsighted political wind direction, and who substantiate and rationalize their chameleon tendencies through the complexities and obscurity of 'spin'. If the political prize is large enough 'spin doctors' appear to cleverly convolute a political premise to the point of hopeless obscurity. Pretty soon our minds are filled with straws of wheat swirling around in a cyclonic vortex from which we must attempt to chaff out a needle. Each political side, individually and collectively, and the multitude of splintered factions and sub-factions, promote their agenda and version of reality defended vehemently and explained esoterically by incessant and incomprehensible nuances resembling everything except the truth. Question the motives, and certainly the veracity, of anyone who spends a hundred million dollars or more to procure a position that carries a four year tenure and renders an annual salary of $400,000. Such is the nature of politics and politicians, and today's elections. Presumed necessities I suppose, but superficial beauty contests nonetheless. In the reality of business, life, and truth, such ends, notwithstanding the theory of profit and loss, surely do not justify the means. It is not my purpose here to critically throw rocks at our political system. But scrutinizing the veracity of those operating within its realm, vying for approval by pretending to represent our interests, and questioning a group whose only evidence of truth is found written on metaphorical checks dispersed as political payback, exposes merely one example, from many, of man's proclivity to distort or to utterly subvert the truth. Certainly, truthful politicians (and humans) can be found, but where?

Why is the truth so hard for humans to get at? Why is truth so conspicuously missing in man's world? I know I run the risk of portraying myself as a misguided misanthrope or, at best, just a hopeless pessimist, but let's face the truth: we lie to our friends, we lie to our lovers, and we lie to ourselves.

Lies or falsities, exclusively indigenous to the human world, fall into three categories:

1. Black lies- intentional communications of false data, with or without intentions of causing harm, while innately knowing the falsity of the statement. These are made more insidious if told with the intention of doing harm.

2. White lies - often socially accepted statements of falsity intentionally communicated to advance the condition of the perpetrator and, or to enhance the circumstance of the receiver.

3. Withholding the truth - simply put this is the intentional act of withholding or repressing essential information and truth based solely on an earthly, personal agenda and a perceived, ephemeral need, regardless of the detrimental, lasting effect the reticence poses to the withholder or to others. This lie can be as malicious and pernicious as the two preceding.

How many times during the course of the day do humans commit all three types of lies? It has become so commonplace to lie that we often forget we are doing so. It is almost reflexive. However, without a dedication to the truth our spirituality wanes and diminishes. Conversely, commitment to the truth is requisite for spiritual growth. Whatever is false is an illusion, whether perpetrated by us or not. Again, I hate to sound mystical but the discussion is necessary. The physical world is nothing but an illusion and in order to grow in spirit we must transcend this illusionary world and must be determined to seek reality in truth. For without truth our soul's spirit cannot become one with the universe and God. When we die, our soul leaves this world of illusion and returns to the world of the absolute, the world of God. But that is then; this is now. To live truthfully while on earth is to explore and expand the health of our individual essence and serves to improve the collective soul of society. Devoid of truth, the relationship with yourself and others, human and non-human, will remain stale and incomplete. Truth is vibrant, budding and growing; falsity is redundant and stagnant, and creates a world of infertility where the seed of the collective and individual spirit finds fallow ground.

Think for a moment about how much time and energy collectively and individually we spend in all aspects of our physical existence fabricating lies or trying to avoid being duped by them. In a world without falsity, courtrooms would be empty, lawyers' caseload and income would reduce drastically, and politicians would only tell the truth and accurately demonstrate who they really are. Suspicions and subsequent quarrels between lovers would be eliminated, fears and conflicts between friends and foes would be quelled, and the necessity for the National Security Agency would be eliminated. The delusion created by falsity and lies is redundant and mercenary. But I hear your protestations. How can we survive in a society without the escape afforded by an occasional lie? How can we grow financially if we don't occasionally lie, or how will we ascend the corporate ladder of success without uttering a flattering falsity to ourselves or to others once in a while? How can our marriages and relationships with loved ones survive if all we live by and all we express is the naked, unadulterated truth? You protest that black lies, white lies and withholding the truth are sometimes necessary for success, goodwill, diplomacy, and survival. To that I have two comments: the first, hogwash (and I like pigs); the second, consider your dog!

But you say 'such a comparison is unrealistic,' pointing out that dogs aren't saddled with the burden of working for a living. They don't have to survive in the dog-eat-dog (pardon the pun) world we live in. Furthermore, you say 'because of humans, dogs live a simple and sheltered existence'; our world is complex and ominous, our existence and success precarious. I have anticipated your response to the comparison and on the surface your objections and arguments are valid, but only superficially. It is true that a dog's life is not tied to a time clock, nor do they endure the mental and physical 'slings and arrows' which accompanies the daily grind. They are not required to plan finances around a college education. Their lives don't include a corporate or social ladder they must climb to find success. They are not compelled to solve the conundrum of balancing the checkbook against the quest for self-gratification. They don't have to deal with the expectations and the criticisms of society when failure occurs. Although, I contend the real detriment of failure is the stigma we assign to it which would improve once we realize how to learn and benefit from it.

Sure, our life is extrinsically more complicated than a dog's life, but the complexity is solely our creation. We create it, we perpetuate it, and we expand it. We created it when we first shook our ancestral fist at nature, proclaiming ourselves masters of our domain, transcending the law of nature, and living beyond its tenets. I have said before that God recognizes the complexity caused by our disconnection, and the suffering the separation engenders. Life is hard because we have had a direct hand in causing the difficulty. Complexity breeds confusion and because of confusion bad choices are made. Our sub-conscience, the part of our spirit which remains connected to nature, God, and the natural laws, strains to be heard, but is quelled by our desire to justify all nefarious actions. Subsequently, dishonesty within ourselves is born and is perpetuated. Our society helps generate continuous dishonesty and we become absorbed by it. It is even more discouraging to see society extol the results of dishonesty, applauding its achievements. Being able to dupe another person or entity in a business deal is treated as an achievement and the perpetrator is applauded and deemed a success. Deceit and trickery are glorified in all walks of life: the ends justify the means. It's OK to be dishonest and to get what you want and think you need and deserve, no matter the cost to others. It doesn't matter how you go about it, it doesn't matter what part of yourself you have to abandon - like honesty. It's OK to get something for nothing, that's what is called being slick, and being slick is applauded because it bypasses integrity and takes a short-cut around the effort of, and the spiritual growth resulting from, being honest. Yes, we humans do live in a complex, menacing society: a society that, by our sole design and singular dishonesty becomes more and more ominous day by day.

So what does all this have to do with dogs? The bond between man and dog is no accident; for there are no accidents in the universe. We *need* to be with dogs but, by God's design, dogs *want* to be with us, and they endure despite many of their noble kind suffering the whimsical cruelty or deliberate neglect at the hands of humans. However, they persist by example to hold us to several standards of virtue and one of those virtues is intrinsic honesty. Dogs are our touchstone to honesty and our benchmark of authenticity. It may seem naïvely anthropomorphic (I hate that word for it only has significance as it describes non-living, man-made things) but I challenge you to find a more authentically honest creature, including man, to whom you are associated. Dogs are authentic, honest, and true, strictly adhering to the famous words:

> *"This above all, to thine own self be true.*
> *And it must follow, as the night the day,*
> *Thou canst not be then false to any man."*

No man follows the advice of the Great Bard as does the dog, who unquestionably follows Shakespeare's simple equation-'true to yourself equals true to others'. Unfortunately, humans all too often follow the inverse of the equation: lie to yourself, lie to others. Regrettably, our collective and individual soul is snared and held by the dishonest 'tangled web we weave'. For lying to yourself is the act of withholding the internal truth and inhibiting your true soul. When we hide behind the internal door

133

of dishonesty, we suppress the truth and dim the light of spiritual growth. This causes humans to suffer under one of society's great foibles, one of our most insidious collective diseases, and the origin of all intrinsic dishonesty: repression - repression of emotions, the subversion of intrinsic truth, and the suppression of openness. It is our incessant practice of this repression that engenders our innate dishonesty with ourselves and subsequently with others.

In contrast, dogs can't lie to us or confuse us about their character because dogs can't lie to or hoodwink themselves. They belong to the world of the absolute where deception and dishonesty cannot exist. They visit our world acting as our guide but they belong, in soul and spirit, to the world of nature and God. Their emotions, therefore, are pure, their integrity is uncompromised, and, above all, they are true to their 'self'. Dogs don't hide their emotions or their truth behind a partition; they know who they are and what their truth is. Unlike humans they can't pretend to be something they are not; also, they truly like who they are! Dogs are in touch with their emotions and for them repression of their emotions is impossible; the swinging door to their feelings is always open. In contrast to humans, dogs don't pretend to be happy when they are sad, and they don't pretend to be your friend when they are not. Dogs can't tell you a lie today with the intent on it doing harm to you tomorrow, and they can't tell you a lie today to cover up the lie they told yesterday. If they love you, they immediately adore you, showering you with true emotions while having no compunction or inhibition. If they fear you or feel threatened, they will without apology, openly and frankly snub you and, in some cases, honestly bite you, having no regrets for that truthful action either. What you see, is what you get, because who you see is truly who they are. Candidness invites entry to their essence without barriers; and without barriers, the swinging door to internal truth and emotions is unlocked. With honesty, openness is always manifested, and repression of truth (dishonesty) always disappears; for the two opposites cannot exist simultaneously within the same body. It cannot be otherwise!

When honesty is demonstrated, it will engender demonstration of honesty in return. That is why some of us find it easy to show our true feelings toward a dog. By their honesty, they render us helpless to repress our soul and spirit and consequently our true honesty is revealed. We can't help ourselves; for there is no threat in honesty, only in deceit and pretense. And if we are not threatened, repression wanes and the true essence of our soul's honesty is allowed to flourish. Repression is covert and solitary; conversely, truth and honesty is open and reciprocal, and the defining nature and merit of a dog.

The dog comes to us naturally without any barriers unless, by our cruelty, we cause them to erect defenses. But even in such a case, humans can only temporarily stifle the dog's true nature of openness, for I have witnessed the expression of true goodness and the gracious nature of Greyhounds rescued from the horrific world of cruelty practiced by the humans in the racing business. I have first hand knowledge of demonstrative, true joy openly given by cruelly abused rescued dogs, as my present dog family consists of two of them. Even in cases when the dog comes to us from an abusive background, the true nature of his soul, the true essence of himself, he bears openly for our inspection; if he is given a chance and a kind word. If you look into a dog's eyes, you can look down deep into his soul because what he is on the surface is what he is within, the epitome of TRUTH. Looking into his soul, you are delving into his truth, and he will eagerly reveal his truth to you for he cannot do otherwise. And this is what you will see and this is what he will express:

I cannot lie to you because I cannot lie to myself. I cannot repress my true feelings of joy when you come home after being away from me, neither can I hide the truth of my sadness when you are gone. In truth, I cannot and do not disguise my worship for you. You can be a sinner or saint, a pauper or a prince for it matters not, for the truth of my love cannot be diminished if you are either, for truly I adore you for what you are and in truth I love you in spite of what you are not. Even if you sometimes ridicule me, ignore me or at times treat me harshly the truth of my devotion cannot, and will not, be compromised or truly changed and my true adulation will endure and will even transcend the pain you may cause. Even if your harshness leads to my physical demise, the truth of my love for you remains, unwavering. All of this is true and shall be so forever as long as I am with you, and even when I am not. I merely ask that during your busy life you show kindness and truth to me once in awhile. Walk with me for just a time and experience my truth. But if you do not, if you ignore me, or you choose to be unkind and dishonest, I will not desert you, for in truth, I cannot. I will wait patiently as you search for yourself, knowing one day you cannot refuse to return to the truth I so freely give. We will again unite, both rejoicing and sharing in our joy, truth, and love. And with your return, you will find me dogged in my devotion, you will realize my steadfast truth; and, as you see the goodness and truthfulness of my soul, you will then also recognize my unwavering belief in the goodness and truthfulness of yours.

In all of mankind's history on earth, only One has lived and died offering the same such TRUTH.

So the next time you consider it expedient to your success or necessary to your well being to lie to others or to yourself, or repress your truth, or hide behind dishonesty... consider your dog!

Chapter 19

LOVE

"Love is the ultimate reality. It is the only. The all."
                                    "Conversations With God"

Up to this point the dog's four virtues have been presented: humanity, forgiveness, tolerance, and loyalty. And two of his greatest messages have been exposed- joy and truth. All of these need no reciprocation from humans, for the dog's inherent nature stimulates the demonstration of these virtues and his mission is to deliver the messages. The dog will offer his forgiveness without humans returning the virtue. Loyalty is so basic to the dog's nature that he remains so even if shunned or abandoned by his human keeper. Humility and humanity are demonstrated with or without accolades or rewards. And, devoid of ego, their unprejudicial attitude is so elemental that the dog knows no other alternative. His joy is so natural its repression is unnatural. Truth is so crucial to his nature that he cannot be dishonest. So what about love?

Love is the most magnificent gift demonstrated and the most important message delivered by the dog. Considering the importance of the subject of this chapter, I planned to begin it by offering a definition, for lack of a better word; sort of an explanation, a description of the dog's inherent love for us which is clearly unmatched by any other creature on earth, including such that is offered in this regard by our own species. A love, in its truth and by its demonstration, that is closer to unconditional love as we will find existing in this physical world. Many anecdotal examples of the dog's love are available for report, and many stories could be recounted attesting to and substantiating the dog's worth in this regard. But the dog offers a uniquely sublime love and I wanted this chapter to explain its sublimity, and not just offer conventional, although impressive, anecdotal accounts, many of which I experience daily from my own. In short, it would be too easy and mundane to explain their superlative and unique love by using anecdotal technique, and in some ways this method might narrow the magnitude of it. So I figured the greatness of their love deserved, if not a better approach, at least a different one. So I went looking for terms to describe and explain their love. Expressions that would measure up, or were at least commensurate with the magnificence of its nature.

Love unexplained

I had anticipated this chapter since I began writing the prologue of this book. I knew this chapter was going to be the big one, the grandest, and the best of all because love itself is such. And I predicted it would be the easiest to write. The word love is so powerful, it is so rich and resplendent; so engrossing with so much to write, how could I fail to get at its meaning and its characteristics as it exists in a dog's world. *Boy was I in for a surprise.*

With the previous chapters completed, edited, revised and out of the way, I now cleared my mind for the grand finale, the 'coup de grace'. The hard part was over, now it was down-hill as I approached the easiest part of all. With my pen ready on a quiet, late-winter morning, I began with eager anticipation of the coming spring and the beginning of this chapter. Then---nothing, but then--- everything! As I patiently waited for the proper words to begin flowing into my mind, the dam broke and a thunderous avalanche swept my way, taking me wherever it desired, in all different directions and yet nowhere. It raged upon me, drowning me. I truly hate extended metaphors but I can't explain what occurred any more accurately. I was powerless against its control. Every time I thought I had overcome its force and began feebly to explain the word love, my mind was swept away by the sheer magnitude of its power and its mystique. I tried to regain control and my composure; but after reading the numerous drafts, I realized they represented nothing but shaky and unstable life rafts. I abandoned them only to be grabbed again by the torrential power of the word. I was battered and exhausted and I eventually began to doubt that this book was going to be finished at all. Without this chapter, the book would fail altogether and thus I would fail the dog. I gave up. After many attempts to write this chapter, disappointed and disillusioned, I abandoned it. Over the next few weeks an inexorable force within compelled me to continue to write this chapter, and it could not be quelled. And I started again.

In my feeble human attempt to define the love of the dog I had initially began my many now defunct, trashed chapters by using human definitions, human concepts, and human perceptions of the word. The crux of the problem came to light. All of the study and reading I had done concerning the word love over the years, and all of my thoughts and perception of the word were derived from thoughts and words of other humans. Explanations offered by experts - like Freud, Jung, and M. Scott Peck, just to name a few - had bombarded, battered and exhausted my limited mental capacity. There is no shortage of material to be considered when studying human love and trying to get at its meaning. Psychiatrists dissect it, examine it, explain it, and create diseases for it; and then attempt to cure it. Philosophers ponder it, compound it, and confuse it for everyone who is not of their breed. Humans contaminate the term love and weigh it down with human pollution.

To be sure, love is an abstract term. And being abstract, it can be difficult for most humans, including me, to grasp, to hold, and to define. It's not that we haven't tried. I doubt that any other term, any other word, or any other emotion has been dissected, examined, explained, or defined quite as often and with as much enthusiasm. But human perception of this word is vastly complicated. Love certainly is a powerful word and an incredible idea, but an inscrutable abstraction for humans, with as many nuances and definitions as there are idiosyncrasies of the human psyche. And therein lays the problem. We have so complicated the term and impregnated it with our ego that the true meaning of the word and the emotion seems hopelessly lost. We blame it, we transform it, and we manipulate it to fit our standards, and continually revise it to meet our psychological needs. We have so complicated the term because of our disconnection with the universe and God. A separation started thousands of years ago when we first shook our fist at nature, egotistically erecting our platform of separateness from all things natural and truly spiritual. We are not one with the universe; we are not one unto ourselves. Our scientists, psychologists, and philosophers perpetuate this separateness by producing enlightening arguments and explanations of our behavior and emotions, explaining love in strict terms of I and we. They define love strictly in human terms delivering it into the realm of our ego, explaining it and substantiating it by all things human. Psychiatrists and psychoanalysts have reasoned all types of love into existence. There is unrequited love, which according to them causes all sorts of maladies of the mind. They explain that love which seeks to control another is insidious to the controller and the controlled, causing physical and, or, mental abuse. We have dependent love, which they explain is not really love at all; for dependent love allows abuse by the person upon whom the dependent one relies on the most. Falling in love or the pursuit of sexual gratification and procreation is an altogether different type of love, but yet not really love at all.

They further substantiate our separateness from all other creatures by bringing into their discussions of love the term of cathexis: the type of love by which we encompass another person's spiritual development into our own thus expanding our ego boundaries, becoming one with another human. But they go on to explain that we can cathect another person into our being, but sometimes that isn't love - merely cathecting. We can cathect objects like money, or we can cathect success, gambling, even a *dog* but this is not love because we cathect these things without the purpose of expanding the object's spirituality and our own. In other words, cathecting anything inhuman cannot be love because we cannot spiritually enhance ourselves unless we are cathecting or loving another *human*, because true love is attained only through human-to-human relationships. However, this definition is purely defined in human terms. In other words, love is strictly a human-to-human concept. They justify their position by saying communication and language is requisite to producing love. Therefore, since humans are the only creatures on earth that share language and are the exclusive participants in communication, all other creatures are left in the void. Such are the teachings of our mainstream psychiatrists, and psychotherapists to whom most humans in their daily lives have become so addicted. It is all about the **Us**, the **I**.

All of this becomes pretty confusing to one who doesn't have a Ph.D. at the end of his name. So as we read all the scientific treatises, all the medical publications, and all the articles ever written explaining what love is and what love is not, how much have we progressed in our understanding of the term? Most of our scientists, politicians and therapists in order to reach the pinnacle of success, pander to the group or species that sends success their way.

Moreover, humans reward the pandering experts with our undivided attention, showering them with the praise of credulity. And I joined them! All this has complicated our human existence and has reduced it to the realm of the 'I' to the point that because of our ego we can't even explain, succinctly and with clarity, the term love.

Psychiatrists and psychoanalysts define love in human terms with human diseases, contaminating the feeling with words and feeble explanations, and shrouding it in a preponderance of language and theory. The word conjures up more discussions, contains more definitions, casts more shadows, and gives off more nuances than any other human word. The abstract word, love, the most powerful force in the entire universe, *is the mother* of all abstract terms and the mother of all magnets, attracting numerous and futile attempts to define it, explain it, and understand it. Our language has become so complex and replete, but, being the most inefficient mode of communication, is inadequate and fails miserably when we attempt to define, give, receive, or even recognize love. We literally beat the poor word to death. The grandest most powerful force on earth, and in the universe, literally has been sent into oblivion. Humans, caught up in the pretense of erroneous definitions and confused by all the rhetoric, abuse the word, mangling its meaning to the point beyond recognition. When the vast majority of us say "I love you", what does it mean? Those three words actually mean in human terms what can you do for me! Even some of the most perennial relationships and marriages are tainted with selfishness. We humans extol this selfishness by calling it 'give **and take**' and consider it necessary to a lasting, loving relationship.

When it came down to my expression and description of the word love as it applies to this book and its protagonist, I realized that no human thoughts, words, definitions, or illusions of the word would suffice and in fact did nothing but complicate and augment the avalanche of conflicting ideas and emotions brought forth only in human terms. There are no words in the human language, no thought processes capable of describing the power of the love contained in a dog. No human explanation and description can match the nobility of the dog's pure and incomprehensible demonstration of the term. For human terms and descriptions of the word only constrict a dog's love and contaminate it with human diseases. All that I had perceived would be written in this chapter was erroneously extrapolated from human minds, including my own. And, although the greatest and most astute were consulted for their explanation, it wasn't measuring up. 'I was looking for love in all the wrong places'.

As a last gasp and eager for a lucid, less convoluted explanation than those of the pundits, (and my own) I turned to a group of friends and relatives, hoping for feedback to help me get back on track with this chapter. I approached them with a few questions. Some in the group were strictly religious and some not, some with and some without connections with dogs. The first question: what is love? All had their perceptions and shared them gladly. Some gave perceptions that were well thought out, yet some, reeling from the sheer magnitude of the question, fumbled around feebly trying to describe it. And all were eager to answer the second question: can we comprehend the depth and magnitude of God's love; can we understand it, explain it, and try to emulate it? Many exclaimed, 'sure we can'! Then I asked a simple, yet complex, question. 'Why can *all* humans go to what we understand to be heaven; or, in other words, return to the Creator, as His love never abandons us?' (I intentionally specified humans so as not to complicate the issue.) Some were aghast, completely stunned by the words of the question. Some vehemently argued that '*not all humans*' are allowed in heaven. However, they were forced to admit, grudgingly, that His love and forgiveness never fails, and He *never* abandons us. Even with that admission, most refused to admit to, and failed to realize, the contradiction inherent in their argument for exclusion. The more thoughtful pondered the question, waffled back and forth with conflicting responses, and finally, and honestly, admitted that they didn't know the answer. And that's precisely my point and precisely why I had such a hard time attempting to explain the word love as it exists in a dog's world.

Man over the ages has defined God and His love in man's terms. Therefore, everything from His appearance to His preferences has been portrayed through man's perception. But we can't determine in our feeble mind who or what God is or what He perceives, what He looks like, or the magnitude of *His love*. We attempt to explain it the best way we know how; we explain it using human terms and perceptions. Is all we know about God an illusion, merely a reflection of ourselves emanating from the mirror of human ego? If we cannot understand God except by the light of our own mere reflection, then our understanding is truly flawed. And so it follows that our concept of the creation and the goodness of our soul is flawed. Furthermore, so is our understanding of the Creator's love, the perception of which, clouded by such an illusion, remains elusive. But we know that His love is sublime, constant, and forgiving. Not by our reflection of ourselves, but by the manifestation of His presence in all things human and nonhuman. For all that God has created demonstrates His perfection and love, *and to Him all creations in their perfection must return.* His creations are exquisite and true and so is His love, which is incomprehensible to our human mind. In all creations of his hand perfection is evident, but yet inscrutable and sometimes mysterious. And the perfection of His love is likewise mysterious, inscrutable, and omnipresent. We know He is here with us for He exists in every breath of the wind and every hue of the sky, every spectrum of color in a rainbow, in the green, amber, and brown of the grass and trees. He exists in every spring blossom and He resides in every falling autumn leaf. He *is* every creation we see, from the furthest star in the universe, to the closeness of the spirit of our soul. And so it is with all, including the dog, most especially the dog who represents tangible evidence of God's humanity, forgiveness, tolerance, loyalty, truth, and love. The dog's inscrutable love builds the bridge to God and by the dog's love we are able to look beyond the reflection of God we see in the mirror. To go beyond this two-dimensional concept is to find His truth and love. And to experience this love all we have to do is to reach out and touch the soul of a dog, which he reveals so eagerly. Such an easy thing to do, yet so magnificent. For within him we find the tangible essence of godliness. Such is the wonderful accessibility of the gifts inherent in the dog: the joy, the truth, and most especially the love. To touch a dog is to feel his joy, truth and Love, and the love we find within is truly godly: as close to God's love as we will find on earth!

With that said, I realize that in previous chapters I already described the love of a dog, although feebly; for the extent and magnificence of the dog's love cannot be explained with words. Human language is inherently inadequate, for not even words written by a literary genius could convincingly portray or sufficiently explain the majestic splendor of their unconditional love. Yet, befittingly, the dogs themselves demonstrate their love more accurately than I ever could and they do so by proving the extent and magnitude of the six gifts already expressed by them. Not just in the previous chapters of this book, but in all theaters of our lives. In every place they exist, they offer their virtues of unselfish *humility and humanity*, their unfaltering *forgiveness*, their *unprejudiced heart*, their undying *loyalty*, their *joy,* and their *truth*. All unmatched by any creature on earth, including man. If my feeble efforts in this book fall short of providing a clear, true description of their wonderful nature and the magnificence of their gifts so graciously offered, I remain confident the dog's humble demonstration of these six virtues surpasses and pales any human attempt to portray them adequately. And the dogs do so without saying a word. Furthermore, what is real love if not the true, gratuitous offering of these virtues? And, without uttering a single word, their transcendent gift of the *seventh*, and the supremacy of it, is explained and defined by the true, gratuitous demonstration of their six virtues. The sum of which is sublime *Love*.

A dog's sublime love belongs to another realm, for it cannot be found or duplicated in this one. Therefore, a dog's love cannot be dissected, examined, or explained by humans with human language and in human terms, *and neither can God's!*

Unfortunately, our apathetic reciprocation of the dog's love parallels our self-absorbed attitude toward God. Dogs love us more than we love ourselves, far more than we love each other, and regrettably more than we love him. Luckily for us, the dog's Love is as *near* to unconditional as we shall find in this world and as close to the *true* unconditional One we find coming from the next. And a dog's love is similarly inscrutable and indefinable. For a dog's love can be described solely by the *words* of One, and surpassed in eminence and demonstration only by the Same One: the One who instilled it - their Creator.

Ironically, after almost four weeks of struggling to complete this chapter, I finally found my way, and finished it on Good Friday, 2007

Chapter 20

SERENDIPITY

"All knowledge, the totality of all questions and answers, is contained in the dog."

Franz Kafka, "Investigations of a Dog"

Have you ever looked to the sky on a clear, moonless night observing millions of twinkling needles of light shinning from far-off distant corners of the universe? Your eyes catch a faint glimpse of a distant point of light but as you attempt to focus it into view, it disappears from sight. As you look away slightly it reappears in view, but as you attempt to recapture its focus, it fades again to obscurity.

Man's journey on his evolutionary path contains a phenomena or miracle: the gift of Serendipity: 'the gift of finding valuable or agreeable things not sought for.' Acting against the gift of serendipity, humans eagerly practice a transfixing tendency commonly referred to as Entity-Thinking: The desire to know the location and identity of things like love and God, compelling us to ascertain the true nature of all things mysterious and separate. On the beneficial side of the equation, this tendency generates the hard work and dedication necessary for discovery and enlightenment. But on the other side, sometimes this tendency interferes with our awareness of serendipitous gifts, foiling our capacity to comprehend fully the presentation and realization of discovery. The concept of grace, the reward of evolutionary progression, remains akin to the vanishing star of light in the night sky, as do the concepts of love and God. Sometimes we look too intensely, become so absorbed that we miss the discovery altogether. This is when the miracle and gift of serendipity happens, and the dog's role in the presentation of the gift becomes evident.

Man has a deep, compelling need to be loved, to be worthy, to be treasured by someone, to be the center of someone's universe. For to love and to be loved is to share the umbrella of love's protection against the inclement weather of life. But many times human to human relationships fail the test of time and constancy mainly because of fear and its offspring – ego. Sometimes lovers are separated physically only in death, and these are the lucky ones; for sometimes love is never found. Yes, the need to love and to be loved is basic and powerful and has been since the beginning of time. And since the beginning of time, man has sought a more perfect love with a mystical being, one offering a supernatural, constant love and protection. A love that even transcends death: and this man calls his god. In some ways the pursuit has been elusive, for man has created many types and species of gods throughout the ages. And the image and specter of God has been viewed by many different worshipers in many different ways, and this we refer to as 'religion'; each one considered inclusively correct, and exclusively separate from others. Hence, history has witnessed the prosecution of *Holy Wars,* as well as the reality of contradiction inherent in the term. Not only has mankind been unable to get on the same page with each other when it comes to finding the right path to the right god, but the image and presence of God in our collective society, and in our individual being, seems to be vanishing from anyone's view.

During the 16th and 17th centuries, mankind in Europe emerged from the Medieval Period, sometimes referred to as the dark ages. A period marked by regressive events like the plague, which killed an estimated twenty-five to thirty million inhabitants of a feudalistic society; a period in which society witnessed few advances in medicine and natural science. A society which strictly adhered to a religious doctrine designed to keep the uneducated and downtrodden masses in check by a hierarchical philosophy which taught that all men, creatures, and things were categorized in a descending order. Each bound to their respective position, and each obligated to fulfill their role according to their own station and rank. At the apex of this doctrine sat the figure of a benevolent yet stern God, the Supreme Being responsible for man's existence on an earth that was located at the center of the universe. A universe whose order and movement, in keeping with the philosophy of the era, obeyed the directives of the hand of God. However, the sociological tenets, and the view of the physical world were about to change, and so would the perception and location of God.

Copernicus, Galileo, Kepler, and Sir Isaac Newton, all regarded now as great scientists of the 'Age of Enlightenment', advanced theories that challenged the firmly entrenched, age-old concept of the universe. And armed with newly formed scientific methods of evidence,

153

they would turn the perception of the universe topsy-turvy and question God's, as well as man's, position and purpose in it. Copernicus was first to challenge the earth's position at the center of the universe by postulating the earth, as well as the other planets, revolved in orbit around the sun. Galileo, looking through his telescope, noticed movement of the other planets and witnessed moons moving in orbit around Jupiter. Kepler, believing the orbit of planets was elliptical, advanced mathematical equations explaining the relationship between a planet's distance from the sun and the duration of its orbit around it. Newton explained the properties of gravity and through equations of calculus, which he invented, he described this force of gravity at work holding the planets in an orderly, predictable orbit around the sun. In light of these advances, eventually society came to view the earth (and man) no longer as the center of the universe. It became an accepted belief that the earth, like other planets, moved in a predictable orbit which adhered to explainable forces independent from the benevolent direction of God. This is not a history book, but the importance of such a discussion here is to show our concept of God along with our advancement as a species has gone through many stages along the path of our evolution. And the 'Age of Enlightenment' indicates a prime example of the major changes in our perception of God as well as ourselves along this path. For no longer could man claim to exist at the center of the universe, no longer could he declare to be under the protection and patronage of a benevolent God. We were on our own. Some men of the age bemoaned these scientific discoveries believing God had been displaced from the heavens and removed as the influence and inspiration for leading a moral life. Man, no longer at the center of the universe, was merely an insignificant denizen inhabiting a godless world and whose life, devoid of purpose, became meaningless. The momentous discoveries and the devastating theories of science advanced during that time are regarded as inconsequential facts by any sixth-grader today; as is the fact that gods do not direct the affairs of man from Mount Olympus.

Since the seventeenth century, science and its tools have advanced exponentially, as has our society. Scientists of our era looking through another telescope, the Hubbell, state they see evidence of the universe's creation that occurred somewhere about fourteen billion years ago. Particles of dust and gases existing within what they label as a 'singularity,' the origin and nature of which remains unknown, came under extreme pressure from an intense gravitational force the likes of which is difficult to comprehend. From this action, a type of an explosion or implosion ensued creating intense heat, anti-matter, and matter. From matter, elemental atoms were formed which coalesced into larger forms creating, as the process cooled, the billions of planets and suns which are continually moving outward from the point of the initial explosion, eventually developing into the universe we know today. Before the 'Big Bang' nothing existed - nothing except a thing called a 'singularity,' the origin and nature of which remains a complete mystery, unknown to science. After the explosion, there was something: the thing we call our universe. And together we exist on our planet called earth, upon which we cohabit with all other incredible creatures and things. A unique world held in orbit around a phenomenal sun, clustered together with several billion other clusters comprising our galaxy which together with billions of others are contained inside an expanding universe that began as an immeasurable, inconceivable, baffling thing called a 'singularity' which mysteriously appeared from nothing comprehendible, for reasons yet determined, fourteen billion years ago.

The majority in the scientific community consider the Big Bang theory indisputable fact. They claim evidence of the initial implosion is viewable through the Hubbell telescope. They support their theory by pointing to the discovery of elemental atoms found in other planets matching those found on our own. They state the bang theory and evolution of the universe adheres and conforms to the 'Second Law of Thermodynamics', and other scientific premises and equations too obtuse and lengthy for discussion in a book about dogs. Its brief mention is necessary only to beg a plethora of questions: Does this scientifically accepted theory further push the existence of man into obscurity, reducing his significance to a minimum, and God's existence into oblivion? And if it does, if it is proven to be fact (as were those during the Age of Enlightenment) and not just a well-explained scientific theory, then what is to become of man's journey of evolution? What would be the point in striving toward a kinder, gentler nature, or what purpose is served by following a life in awareness of God if He doesn't exist? What use does any life form, ours or that of any other species that originated from particles of dust and ethereal gases, have for such a thing like love? How did love, inborn to our 'center of being', originate from and evolve out of dust and gas in the first place? And the most salient question of all: Does God exist - is man truly alone in this vast universe? A fearful question to say the least! Some humans, as they did in the seventeenth century, find support from science for the Creation, some do not. However, one thing is certain: the formation of the universe, the Bang, in the opinion of scientists and theologians alike, was a supernatural event, and both further agree that a mysterious force exists outside the realm of present limits of human understanding. But what *is* this inscrutable force?

Only two emotions exist: fear and love. We know fear exists. Its manifestation pervades and permeates our collective and individual being, emanating from within and imposed on it from without. But who creates fear? Simple. Man is the creator of fear, and fear is the source of all other malicious and destructive emotions of the physical world. But what of love, the unconditional kind? Unlike fear, man is not the first source of love; it must come from another source. But if God is forced into oblivion by science, how can we find its origin, its source? Who or what is the 'First Source' of love's existence? The empirical scientists studying the mind would state that man creates love as the antithesis to fear, but their statement remains only hypothetical. Although science can observe the many manifestations and variations of *human love*, create and label diseases of it, and recommend cures for it, they can't explain the origin of the pure form of it. They can't view the creation of it through a telescope or a microscope and discern its point of initial existence by applying immutable physical laws and equations to substantiate its formation. We know fear exists, and we know the physical universe exists. Man creates fear. And scientists say they are getting close to explaining the creation of the universe. But how can we prove the existence of love or God without proven scientific method of discovery? His existence, and the origin of love, remains as mysterious as the immeasurable and incomprehensible 'singularity', the nature and location of which is indeterminable. We can't touch Him, prove Him, or explain Him. So where do we turn to find Him? Can we find Him, or is He just an illusion, a creation of man originating from man's primary emotion - fear; and the worst genre of fear of all: the fear of being alone and insignificant?

But, again, what about the existence of love, the unconditional kind? If we can't prove the existence of God, how can we be expected to find the First Source of this love, or the origin of our soul? Did these also evolve from the elemental atoms of the bang? If scientific advances in the past four hundred years write God out of the equation of existence, then has not the pure form of love been erased also? Perhaps examining the condition of our world's psyche, we find the alarming, but lucid answer. Should we then revert back to the comforting belief of the middle ages, gullibly accepting without question that we, and the earth we stand on, are located at the center of the universe? Our evolution as a species demands progression, not regression. Therefore, it is necessary that we consider advances of knowledge and science as a catalyst to our growth rather than an excuse to hide from it. But science and its pursuit to discover and explain the physical world is not complete unless simultaneously we discover the awareness of the center of our being. The beginning of awareness can only be found if we start the journey on our evolutionary path, the starting line of which is camouflaged not by its nature, but rather by ours. But where do we turn for evidence of God's love and existence and the reason for our journey in the first place? Man's science fails to provide the answer and so does his religion. The cold hard fact is this: if man were not mortal, man's religion and the pursuit of its nature would not exist. But would God? Socrates once wrote that the gods atop Mount Olympus would continue to rule only as long as mortal men allow them to. Nevertheless, mankind is serendipitously compelled toward the pursuit of knowledge in an attempt to find the evidence. We should not fear the pursuit, for it's one of the basic reasons for undertaking the journey: a journey we are forced to take by the same entity Whose existence we seek to verify. Such is our pursuit of a mystery, an unfathomable entity whose location is indeterminable - call it a 'singularity' if you will. And there exists another force at work nudging us to the starting point: one more tangible, more physically available and evident. The dog.

Here's where serendipity comes into play. Man has scoured the universe, searched the heavens, poured over voluminous opinions, created a multitude of religions, and unfortunately fought many wars in an effort to find God and sublime, unconditional love. And, judging from the condition of our collective world today, with apparently little success. So the dog, the most gracious and important serendipitous gift, appears for our discovery and acceptance. Many times this gift is ignored. But on man's collective and individual journey on the path of evolution, serendipity is at work more than we realize. Many gifts are placed in front of man only to be ignored as most of us just are trying to keep up with the blurring events of our complex life. A complex life compounded by fear and its offspring - ego. An individual may spend years pursuing knowledge in the quest to solve the secrets of the universe, a cure for polio, or to find the true essence of his soul through grace and love. In all courses of study and pursuit of knowledge, in all theatres of life, serendipitous gifts are offered along the path and often discovered quite by accident as events unfold revealing answers at a time when one least expects the epiphany. And so it is with our discovery of the serendipitous dog.

We need the serendipitous gift of the dog and his guidance on our journey to help us unwind the serpentine path with many false detours. His guidance clears our focus allowing us to see the far off needle of vanishing light that disappears from our view, as we remain transfixed, yet blind. If you remember in Chapter 11, 'Stages…And Beyond', I mentioned that the dog's goodness is seldom recognized except by bits and pieces of the puzzle, little slices of the lessons, tiny but indelible black-and-white snapshots of the panoramic picture yet to be discovered. Someday, as we behold the true nature of the dog, mysteriously and serendipitously these snapshots come together, revealing a beautiful tapestry of the promise the journey holds. By manifestations of the dog's virtues, we witness the true demonstration of his gifts and, most importantly, we recognize the existence of God, who is revealed as the only possible origin of the dog's virtues and truths. From dogs, we learn the true meaning of humility and humanity. We learn the value of unfailing forgiveness, we recognize and praise them for their unprejudicial tolerance, and we respect and treasure their undying loyalty. We participate and reciprocate in their unfettered joy, we recognize the untainted truth of their soul and, comparing it to our own, find ours lacking. And we feel their unconditional love, recognizing it unparalleled and unsurpassed by any we can find or imagine in this physical world. Through the tangible existence of the dog, the presence and reality of God is unquestionably evident. For who is the giver, the 'First Source', of the virtues demonstrated by dogs, if not God? Man cannot be the first source! Since man, struck by ego, has long since forgotten he inherently possesses such virtues by creation, necessitating man's evolutionary journey to reconnect to the essence of his spirit in order to find them again. Nor can they originate from elemental atoms, nor particles of dust and gases placed under extreme gravitational pressure, the likes of which are incomprehensible. Nor can they originate from the single cell membrane of a paramecium. Only One can and must be the first source, because....

161

The essence of the dog's virtues must be instilled by a sublime, supernatural source; because, information must be transmitted from and taught by a source which not only inherently holds the information, but also, and most importantly, demonstrates and personifies it.

The Essence of a Dog

God's true essence, not man's erroneous image of Him, is contained within the dog. Like God, the dog transcends the boundaries of man's constructed religions and prejudice. A Jewish dog is the same dog of Islam, the same dog of Buddhism, the same dog of Christianity constantly demonstrating and teaching the same immutable virtues of humility, forgiveness, tolerance, loyalty, joy, truth, and love to all, regardless of man's religion. These seven essential truths are from God; virtues unfailingly practiced by dogs for the past one hundred thousand years. And like God, the mysterious Entity we so desperately seek, the dog remains indisputably unaltered by man's religion and perception. As we *all* listen to the quiet goodness of the dog's soul, we strive to emulate his virtues, as he makes us aware of *our* own. With this awareness serendipitously revealed, we *all* again feel we are at the center of the universe and the evolution of our being has meaning again. We are not alone in a cold, dark godless world. We *all* are the center of the dog's universe, and through them we realize that we *all* remain at the center of God's, regardless of the science of Copernicus, Galileo, and Newton, regardless of which religion of man we follow, all which pale in comparison to the dog's fundamental virtues. As the serendipitous gifts they bring become obvious, we *all* strive to share the protective umbrella of *unconditional love* they offer, knowing that the reward at the end of our journey will contain the manifestation of this love by the One who created it. Along the way of the journey, the dogs sniff out the serendipitous gifts camouflaged and hidden from our view, gifts we humanly miss: precious nuggets of the golden lessons of virtue, theirs and ours, which remain hidden from our view obscured by clouds of ego and fear. With our eyes constantly on the lookout for danger, and our minds preoccupied with ego, we look past these gifts, missing them altogether. The dog's sense of purity and goodness tenderly pulls at the leash which connects our two souls. Gently they nudge us to discover serendipitous gold nuggets of life. They lead us to recognize the sublime lessons of their joy, truth, and love. And they guide us by their inherent virtues of humility and humanity, forgiveness, unprejudicial tolerance, and loyalty. And through them we find nutrients for our soul, nourishment for the center of our being. We store these golden gifts in the pocket of our soul and become rich beyond all the measure of wealth in the physical world. Such are the serendipitous discoveries to which the noble dog leads us as they demonstrate without question that they are the most magnificent gift God sends our way.

But most importantly, they lead us by example to the true awareness of God's vibrant essence and existence. An existence not forced into oblivion and a spirit easily observed in the essence and gifts of the *dog*, who serendipitously appeared one-hundred thousand years ago from an aberration of the evolutionary process instigated by a mysterious force. A force Whose location is no longer indeterminable; the existence of Whom is now made evident and palpable through the presence of the dog. By their unpolluted example of purity, they humbly nudge us to begin our journey, loyally walk with us on it, truthfully guide us around its barriers, and joyfully lead us to its destination: the serendipitous gift of grace and unconditional love. Although some may leave to join others who came before them, they all will wait for us at our destination, remaining at our journey's end together, and rejoicing in our reward. Such is the truth and nature of God's most precious gift and virtuous teacher. And as we greet them at our journey's end, they will hold us close, truly calling us their own.

Because... such is the nature of God, **such is the essence of a dog.**

Chapter 21

THE CRITTERS ARE RESPONSIBLE !

". . .you must turn aside the teachings of your well-meaning but misinformed, worldly tutors, and hear the teachings of those whose wisdom comes from another source".

"Conversations With God"

As I said in the beginning, this book is about a journey - yours not mine, but that statement is not quite true. I hate to bring doubt into this writing at this late juncture, so let me explain. This book *is* about your journey, and its path is up to you. But I wrote it because I was forced to by an elite group who compelled me to take on the daunting task and I had very little choice in the matter. The creation of a book, one that is coherent, sensible, truthful, and appealing might not pose an intimidating task for a literary genius, or a learned scholar, or even an astute politician or ex-president, some of whom even pay other people to do the hard work of mechanically writing the book for them. I am none of the above so at times I was overwhelmed by it. Yet, I did have help. Anyone who writes a book has help in one way or another, for *'no man is an island, entire within himself'*. And while intimidating as this book was for me to complete, I had help from the same critters who forced me to begin it in the first place. All books are creations and reflections of manifestations of events that at one time have occurred around or within the author, happening to, or within - maybe both. My feeble effort with this book is no different in this regard. The purpose for my effort is to explain the result of a journey I started in 1959, with many, many episodes and dynamic manifestations too numerous to list. And, in keeping with this book's purpose, had no place in it, except to mention what was and is the cause of its creation; a creation or writing that proved sometimes very arduous. It would have been easier had I bored you with all the experiences and all the enlightenments revealed to me by my dogs on this journey. Yes, a lot easier. Had I done so this book would have been not only simple to write but very long indeed; and that would have been a mistake. Sometimes a long-winded, self-absorbed story does little to capture an audience, inviting introspection; and rarely does such a work survive in memory. In 1863, a popular and astute orator of the day, Edwin Everett, delivered a long, pompous speech to a large audience on hand to dedicate a cemetery. Although the ostentatious harangue contained useful commentary about the trying times of the era and concerned ongoing tumultuous events, it was two hours long and obviously very boring. No one remembers that speech and newspaper reports of the day quickly dropped its contents, as did the people in attendance who forgot its words simultaneously with its deliverance. But what followed Everett's long harangue is remembered to this day and will be for all ages. The four and one-half minute speech delivered by Lincoln at Gettysburg lives on to this day, remembered for its truth, content, and genius of brevity. Not that this humble book contains such genius, but it does contain truth, and I sincerely hope its contents have not been boring; and, the premise, hopefully stimulating interest and inspiring introspection, will not soon be forgotten. In addition, I hope the main character will be remembered as God's most precious gift, true messengers of His joy, truth, and love; and will be *"held close by you, truly calling them your own"*

The critters who made me do it.

All eleven dogs in my immediate dog family, present or past, have in their own way walked with me through life as my guide. Each in their own way contributing their portions of the message; and every one, in their unique way, aiding me in the direction of my path. The delivery of their messages varied in style, and their presentations were as unique as their personalities. Although different in style, they all remained constant in virtue, consistently epitomizing the attributes of humility, forgiveness, tolerance, and loyalty, while demonstrating and exemplifying joy, truth, and love. Smokey was a strong independent, courageous guide, forceful in purpose. The right dog at the right time for an egocentric, wayward child. Jock was the steady, indomitable one, never wavering until the end and in realty not even then. Mercedes, 'Sweet Mom', as she became known, was the tender one, and foremost in teaching me love. Portia was the apprehensive clown, joyous and exuberant yet serious when I strayed. Pug taught me loyalty when, for no apparent health reason and at a young age, he left me to join my father exactly three months to the day after he died. Perhaps, he knew my father, who dearly loved him, needed him more than I. Little Girl taught me that suffering through unfortunate events could not quell the sweetness of life, nor did her maladies and disease destroy the sweetness of her essence. Puppy and Little It, the two terribly abused rescued dogs still teach me about forgiveness. Callie Lu is still teaching me about unwavering love and devotion, constantly and quietly always at my side. Sallie Mo, the little baby girl now nine years young, still teaches me about the rejuvenation and continuity of life, the essence of perpetual youth and the exuberance and joy we all could demonstrate by keeping the spirit of youth while growing old and wise. All have demonstrated their messages and their virtues and each has contributed to my progression on my journey, keeping me on the right path, and lighting my way.

But Brutus, the most noble and kind of all my companions, brought me to this book. On November 4, 2002, Brutus died after a long-developing malady. The nature of which at his age was untreatable, and the effects of which really didn't become obvious until the early summer of that year. He died at the young age of sixteen years-six months. Many prominent and astute conventional and holistic veterinarians were visited and consulted in order to make his remaining time on earth as pleasant as possible. His death was quiet, but the aftermath was thunderous. His death left behind a very distraught human. He was the firstborn of Mercedes' pups and the last to leave. Trying to cope with his departure, I began taking long meditative walks alone in the woods, something that I hadn't done in thirty-five years. I began reading everything from Shamanism, Buddhism, the writings of Gandhi, the Toltec teachings and more; on I went to the Bible, and on to Freud and other scientists of the mind, on to the great philosophers and humanitarians from Socrates to Albert Schweitzer, and on to new age writings of psychics and clairvoyants. All avenues were explored and searched in an attempt to find solace. Also, close friends admonished me for my depth of despair over the loss of *just a dog'*.

I had not maintained a spiritual connection of any type since my late teens when I rebelled against a strict religious upbringing and a flawed human interpretation of spirituality. Consequently, for many years I lived my life without comfort of such things spiritual in times of deep despair and this time more than any in my life was the most desolate. Even through the years of disconnection, I guess I still had a deep subconscious yearning to know and discover what I had been missing. On the other hand, perhaps I needed to find out if I had missed anything at all. With his death, Brutus led me on a path of discovering myself within, and the journey continues. For along the path, unknowingly started years ago, I had always recognized the inherent goodness and godlike qualities of the dog. However, I was out of touch with the source of the dog's goodness and godliness. I was unaware of the origin of his traits because I remained unaware of God. As I have said, I am not a holy man and I certainly had not lived my life in pursuit of sainthood. However, those who have speak of God's unconditional love for all creatures and report evidence of His glory demonstrated by humanity, forgiveness, tolerance, loyalty, joy, truth and love. But I had not experienced grand visions of God and had no religious epiphany that accompanies such a vision. I had not experienced a near-death incident allowing me to see the face and feel the love of our Creator. I am not a master and I can't lay claim to visions caused by living an ascetic life, nor am I a psychic having talents allowing me to divine the supernatural. Where was I to turn to find the truth? Who owns the truth about God? Many times I asked these questions over the last few years, and in my effort to find the answer I immersed myself in reading man's works and words claiming to hold the truth, reading everything from the Bible to new age works of the likes of Sylvia Browne; but all seemed to fall short of the mark.

No grand visions of God had appeared before me, but out of nowhere, serendipitously, it hit me. In fact…I truly had! Through all the searching, all the reading, and all the questions I asked and all the satisfactory answers I failed to truly receive; as I lost my way, my mind befuddled by all the inadequate information, suddenly all the pieces came together in a tapestry of life and truth, and the enlightenment of the mosaic of true reality was before me. The answer was simple and as close as my feet: The Dog. For if you ignore the fact that the dog doesn't fit our concept of God's regal appearance, and if you look past our human ego, you will discover a creature not separated from us by our feeble prejudice, but rather connected to us by design: God's design. You will then discover a soul of a creature who, like our soul, still belongs to a supernatural realm, but unlike us, simply and honestly, has not lost touch with his Creator. For if you remove the opaque lens of ego covering your minds eye, you will discover the epitome of humility and humanity, unfailing forgiveness, unprejudicial tolerance, undying loyalty, unfettered joy, unfailing truth, and an unconditional love unmatched by any we know in this world. The likeness of which we can only find in One we will know in the next. If you remove our concept of the dog's outward, physical appearance, what and who remains? The answer is clear: visibly, the true appearance and essence of God.

God must exist for His presence is palpable in the tangible being of a Dog.

In conclusion, I must comment on an aspect of this life that seems drastically unfair. The Dog is so perfect in all ways, but his life is so short. On the journey each and every one has led, I have pondered the brevity of this wonderful creature. Their walks with me have been too short, they leave too soon. But I try to realize, through the pain of losing them, they all have accomplished what each had been sent to do. And when their mission is complete, another just as capable appears to continue until we find our way. They are pure, they are of God and they remain one with Him, having no journey they must travel on their way to discover themselves as we do on ours. Luckily, we have them as our guide. So when their job is done, when they have led us in *their* way along our journey, with their mission complete, they return home to receive joyous salutations and a belly rub for a job well done.

Perhaps Jesus did, too.

I end this with a short, beautifully true statement: simple, beautiful, and true like the Dog. It is one my mind reaches for when one of my companions departs from me on our journey and continues on their way to their only *true* Master. It reinforces and reminds them of my gratitude and undying love for them, and reminds me that the Love they so unselfishly offered continues through eternity...

> *"Time is*
> *Too slow for those who wait,*
> *Too swift for those who fear,*
> *Too long for those who grieve,*
> *Too short for those who rejoice.*
> *But for those who love,*
> *Time is eternity."*
>
> Henry van Dyke

A FINAL NOTE

"Nothing is too wonderful to be true if it be consistent with the laws of nature"   Michael Faraday

To walk with dogs and to communicate with their soul is to stroll among the essence of nature, exploring its mysteries and understanding its wonder. For dogs belong to nature's realm, only visiting the human world destined to complete a mission: a mission to introduce us to ourselves again. To take us from where we are to the world from where we came. To lead us out of the false world we have created for ourselves and back to the world of nature where God exists. A world without ego, one devoid of hate, and one that holds truth, joy, and love. A place where evolutionist principles and creationist tenets find common ground. Where evidence and truth combine and meld together the wonder and the magnificence of each group's argument and position. For the *divine intervention* that established the dog-human bond thousands of years ago has provided the gift of the dog. And the *evolution* of our two species, which has brought us, for better and for worse, to where we are today offers the promise of spiritual growth - if we respond to the dog's gentle nudging. As we follow the dog's lead, we soon will be near our destiny and the end of our journey. And as we take the final step crossing the bridge leading to a different world, we will have traveled full circle along our evolutionary path - a path illuminated by the dog's greatest gift - love. Tenaciously, over the millennia the dog has tethered our two souls, entwining them inseparably by his greatest virtue. And as we emulate their virtues, we move closer to the center of our true being and toward the true love instilled within our soul. Here we will find a new world where love has conquered fear, sending *it*, not God, into oblivion; has cleared the clouds of ego; has re-seeded the rebirth of joy; has opened the door to truth; and has built a bridge to a new world order. One we have for so long been destined to regain. A world that holds respect and love for all creations, including ourselves. What would we call such a world to which, by his virtues and with his love, the dog has guided us…Paradise? Such is the divine gift of the dog. Because, his …

"True love is boundless like the ocean and, swelling within one, spreads itself out and, crossing all boundaries and frontiers, envelops the whole world."   Mahatma Gandhi

…and, at our journey's end, as we have followed his virtues and practiced his love, we arrive at our destiny and find our world to be… Heaven.

Remember… *'The completion of a journey of a thousand miles begins with the first step.'* With your dog as your guide take the first step, begin *your* journey and change *your* world. And as we do so individually, so may we together also change the whole of humanity. And so, then, to Paradise we *all* will return.

May Dog guide you, and God bless you, as you travel.

ACKNOWLEDGMENTS AND SUGGESTED READING

Permission to use quoted material from the following books is gratefully acknowledged:

DOGS WHO KNOW WHEN THEIR OWNERS ARE COMING HOME, by Rupert Sheldrake, copyright 1999, reprinted with permission of Three Rivers Press, Random House, New York, NY.

CONVERSATIONS WITH GOD, by Neale Donald Walsch, copyright 1995, used by permission of G. P. Putnam's Sons, a division of Penguin Group (USA) Inc.

BONES WOULD RAIN from the SKY, by Suzanne Clothier, copyright 2002, reprinted with permission of Grand Central Publishing, New York, NY

THE ROAD LESS TRAVELED, by M. Scott Peck, M.D., copyright 1978, reprinted with the permission of Simon & Schuster Adult Publishing Group, New York, NY

LIFE'S GREATEST LESSONS, by Hal Urban, copyright 1997, 2000, 2003, reprinted with the permission of Simon & Schuster Adult Publishing Group, New York, NY

The stories of Joker*, Lord*, Nick* and Bobbie* (Chapter 16) were recounted in my own words and adapted from their stories appearing in DOG MIRACLES, copyright

Additional suggested reading:

A PACK of TWO, by Caroline Knapp, copyright 1998, Random House

DOGS NEVER LIE ABOUT LOVE, by Jeffery Moussaiaff Masson, copyright 1997, Three Rivers Press

GOODBYE, FRIENDS, by Gary Kowalski, copyright 1997, Stillpoint Publishing

ANIMALS AS TEACHERS & HEALERS, by Susan Chernak McElroy, copyright 1996, NewSage Press

THE NATURE of ANIMAL HEALING, by Martin Goldstein DVM, copyright 1999, The Ballantine Publishing Group

CPSIA information can be obtained at www.ICGtesting.com
Printed in the USA
BVOW021554140512

290040BV00005B/3/P